Aldous Huxley's

BRAVE NEW WORLD

NOTES

A CONTEMPORARY
LITERARY VIEWS BOOK

Edited and with an Introduction by
HAROLD BLOOM

3 5 7 9 8 6 4 2

Cover illustration: Photofest

Library of Congress Cataloging-in-Publication Data

Aldous Huxley's Brave new world / edited and with an introduction by Harold Bloom.
p. cm. — (Bloom's Notes)
Includes bibliographical references and index.
Summary: Includes a brief biography of the author, thematic and structural analysis of the work, critical views, and an index of themes and ideas.
ISBN 0-7910-4055-0
1. Huxley, Aldous, 1894–1963. Brave new world. 2. Dystopias in litera-ture. [1. Huxley, Aldous, 1894–1963. Brave new world. 2. English literature—History and criticism.] I. Bloom, Harold. II. Series.
PR6015.U9B65 1996
823'.912—dc20
95-45114
CIP
AC

Chelsea House Publishers
1974 Sproul Road, Suite 400
P.O. Box 914
Broomall, PA 19008-0914

Contents

User's Guide

This volume is designed to present biographical, critical, and bibliographical information on Aldous Huxley and *Brave New World*. Following Harold Bloom's introduction, there appears a detailed biography of the author, discussing the major events in his life and his important literary works. Then follows a thematic and structural analysis of the work, in which significant themes, patterns, and motifs are traced. An annotated list of characters supplies brief information on the chief characters in the work.

A selection of critical extracts, derived from previously published material by leading critics, then follows. The extracts consist of such things as statements by the author on his work, early reviews of the work, and later evaluations down to the present day. The items are arranged chronologically by date of first publication. A bibliography of Huxley's writings (including a complete listing of books he wrote, cowrote, edited, and translated in his lifetime, and important posthumous publications), a list of additional books and articles on him and on *Brave New World,* and an index of themes and ideas conclude the volume.

Harold Bloom is Sterling Professor of the Humanities at Yale University and Henry W. and Albert A. Berg Professor of English at the New York University Graduate School. He is the author of twenty books and the editor of more than thirty anthologies of literature and literary criticism.

Professor Bloom's works include *Shelley's Mythmaking* (1959), *The Visionary Company* (1961), *Blake's Apocalypse* (1963), *Yeats* (1970), *A Map of Misreading* (1975), *Kabbalah and Criticism* (1975), and *Agon: Towards a Theory of Revisionism* (1982). *The Anxiety of Influence* (1973) sets forth Professor Bloom's provocative theory of the literary relationships between the great writers and their predecessors. His most recent books are *The American Religion* (1992) and *The Western Canon* (1994).

Professor Bloom earned his Ph.D. from Yale University in 1955 and has served on the Yale faculty since then. He is a 1985 MacArthur Foundation Award recipient and served as the Charles Eliot Norton Professor of Poetry at Harvard University in 1987–88. He is currently the editor of the Chelsea House series Major Literary Characters and Modern Critical Views, and other Chelsea House series in literary criticism.

Introduction

HAROLD BLOOM

In his "Foreword" to a 1946 edition of *Brave New World* (1931), Aldous Huxley expressed a certain regret that he had written the book when he was an amused, skeptical aesthete rather than the transcendental visionary he had since become. Fifteen years had brought about a world in which there were "only nationalistic radicals of the right and nationalistic radicals of the left," and Huxley surveyed a Europe in ruins after the completion of the Second World War. Huxley himself had found refuge in what he always was to call "the Perennial Philosophy," the religion that is "the conscious and intelligent pursuit of man's Final End, the unitive knowledge of the immanent Tao or Logos, the transcendent godhead or Brahman." As he sadly remarked, he had given his protagonist, the Savage, only two alternatives: to go on living in the Brave New World whose God is Ford (Henry), or to retreat to a primitive Indian village, more human in some ways, but just as lunatic in others. The poor Savage whips himself into the spiritual frenzy that culminates with his hanging himself. Despite Huxley's literary remorse, it seems to me just as well that the book does not end with the Savage saving himself through a mystical contemplation that murmurs "That are Thou" to the Ground of All Being.

A half-century after Huxley's "Foreword," *Brave New World* is at once a bit threadbare, considered strictly as a novel, and more relevant than ever in the era of genetic engineering, virtual reality, and the computer hypertext. Cyberpunk science fiction has nothing to match Huxley's outrageous inventions, and his sexual prophecies have been largely fulfilled. Whether the Third Wave of a Gingrichian future will differ much from Huxley's *Brave New World* seems dubious to me. A new technology founded almost entirely upon information rather than production, at least for the elite, allies Mustapha Mond and Newt Gingrich, whose orphanages doubtless can be geared to the bringing up of Huxley's "Bokanovsky groups." Even Huxley's intimation that "marriage licenses will be sold like dog licenses, good for a period of twelve months," was being seriously considered in California a few years ago. It is true that Huxley expected (and feared) too much from the "peaceful" uses of atomic energy, but that is one of his few failures in secular prophecy. The God of the Christian Coalition may not exactly be Our Ford, but he certainly is the God whose worship assures the world without end of Big Business.

Rereading *Brave New World* for the first time in several decades, I find myself most beguiled by the Savage's passion for Shakespeare, who provides the novel with much more than its title. Huxley, with his own passion for Shakespeare, would not have conceded that Shakespeare could have provided the Savage with an alternative to a choice between an insane utopia and a barbaric lunacy. Doubtless, no one ever has been saved by reading Shakespeare, or by watching him performed, but Shakespeare, more than any other writer, offers a possible wisdom, as well as an education in irony and the powers of language. Huxley wanted his Savage to be a victim or scapegoat, quite possibly for reasons that Huxley himself never understood. *Brave New World,* like Huxley's earlier and better novels *Antic Hay* and *Point Counter Point,* is still a vision of T. S. Eliot's Waste Land, of a world without authentic belief and spiritual values. The author of *Heaven and Hell* and the anthologist of *The Perennial Philosophy* is latent in *Brave New World,* whose Savage dies in order to help persuade Huxley himself that he needs a reconciliation with the mystical Ground of All Being. ❖

Biography of
Aldous Huxley

Aldous Leonard Huxley was born on July 6, 1894, in Godalming in Surrey, England. He came from a family of distinguished scientists and writers: his grandfather was Thomas Henry Huxley, the great proponent of evolution, and his brother was Julian Sorrell Huxley, who became a leading biologist. Aldous attended the Hillside School in Godalming and then entered Eton in 1908, but he was forced to leave in 1910 when he developed a serious eye disease that left him temporarily blind. In 1913 he partially regained his sight and entered Balliol College, Oxford.

Around 1915 Huxley became associated with a circle of writers and intellectuals who gathered at Lady Ottoline Morell's home, Garsington Manor House, near Oxford; here he met T. S. Eliot, Bertrand Russell, Osbert Sitwell, and other figures. After working briefly in the War Office, Huxley graduated from Balliol in 1918 and the next year began teaching at Eton. He was, however, not a success there and decided to become a journalist. Moving to London with his wife Maria Nys, a Belgian refugee whom he had met at Garsington and married in 1919, Huxley wrote articles and reviews for the *Athenaeum* under the pseudonym Autolycus.

Huxley's first two volumes were collections of poetry, but it was his early novels—*Crome Yellow* (1921), *Antic Hay* (1923), and *Those Barren Leaves* (1925)—that brought him to prominence. By 1925 he had also published three volumes of short stories and two volumes of essays. In 1923 Huxley and his wife and son moved to Europe, where they traveled widely in France, Spain, and Italy. A journey around the world in 1925–26 led to the travel book *Jesting Pilate* (1926), just as a later trip to Central America produced *Beyond the Mexique Bay* (1934). *Point Counter Point* (1928) was hailed as a landmark in its incorporation of musical devices into the novel form. Huxley developed a friendship with D. H. Lawrence, and from 1926 until Lawrence's death in 1930 Huxley spent much time looking after him during his illness with tuberculosis; in 1932 he edited Lawrence's letters.

In 1930 Huxley purchased a small house in Sanary, in southern France. It was here that he wrote one of his most celebrated volumes, *Brave New World* (1932), a negative utopia or "dystopia" that depicted a nightmarish vision of the future in which science and technology are used to suppress human freedom.

Huxley became increasingly concerned about the state of civilization as Europe lurched toward war in the later 1930s: he openly espoused pacifism and (in part through the influence of his friend Gerald Heard) grew increasingly interested in mysticism and Eastern philosophy. These tendencies were augmented when he moved to southern California in 1937. With Heard and Christopher Isherwood, Huxley formed the Vedanta Society of Southern California, and his philosophy was embodied in such volumes as *The Perennial Philosophy* (1945) and *Heaven and Hell* (1956).

During World War II Huxley worked as a scenarist in Hollywood, writing the screenplays for such notable films as *Pride and Prejudice* (1941) and *Jane Eyre* (1944). This experience led directly to Huxley's second futuristic novel, *Ape and Essence* (1948), a misanthropic portrait of a postholocaust society written in the form of a screenplay.

In California Huxley associated with Buddhist and Hindu groups, and in the 1950s he experimented with hallucinogenic drugs such as LSD and mescalin, which he wrote about in *The Doors of Perception* (1954). *Brave New World Revisited* (1958), a brief treatise that discusses some of the implications of his earlier novel, continues to be very pessimistic about the future society, particularly in the matters of overpopulation and the threat of totalitarianism. But in *Island* (1962)—the manuscript of which Huxley managed to save when a brush fire destroyed his home and many of his papers in 1961—he presents a positive utopia in which spirituality is developed in conjunction with technology.

Late in life Huxley received many honors, including an award from the American Academy of Letters in 1959 and election as a Companion of Literature of the British Royal Society of Literature in 1962. His wife died in 1955, and the next year he married Laura Archera, a concert violinist. Aldous Huxley died of cancer of the tongue on November 22, 1963, the same day as John F. Kennedy and C. S. Lewis. ❖

Thematic and Structural Analysis

In the **first two chapters** of *Brave New World* the narrator guides our education into the fundamental workings of a future society in which science and sociology have become the same thing. The sentence fragments that begin the novel place the reader at a scene of surprising perspective before a "squat grey building of only thirty-four stories." That the "World State's motto" over the entrance to this building includes the words "hatchery" and "identity" signals a fantasy about paradoxes in which the individual is rendered insignificant by the scale of both the architecture and the World State. We are at a place of progress and inertia, a dystopia, what the Greeks named a "bad place," in the year 632 After Ford. Huxley's satire intends to unsettle a reader's uncritical faith in progress and technology. In this anti-utopian fantasy he imagines a society where even the individual's aesthetic sense is distracted and subsumed.

In the novel's remarkable first full paragraph the narrator invests intangible properties of light with appetite and intention. Pale sunlight "hungrily" seeks human contact, only to be deadened against the tubes of microscopes, transformed by the eye into "buttery" richness. Juxtaposed with the "corpse-coloured" rubber gloves on the hands of the workers, the "luscious" image evokes a sense of decay and unwholesomeness, of something literally unpalatable. The cold of the windows' northern exposure, and the cold in the absence of human touch, is intensified by the fact that this is a fertilizing room, a place of procreation where all intimacy has been obliterated. In this disturbing conflation of sensuous impression and cold sterility Huxley introduces the novel's most compelling theme, that science and technology may displace even the most irreducible of human projects.

The reader moves through these first two chapters with the "troop of newly arrived students" who follow the Director of Hatcheries and Conditioning through the various departments. "I shall begin at the beginning," the D.H.C. announces, in a biblical tone. The students record the words, "straight from the horse's mouth," with the diligence of gospel writers. The "beginning" is a week's supply of ova, purchased from women for "six months' salary" and the "good of Society." The first step in the production of citizens is a financial transaction and a patriotic act.

Bokanovsky's Process is a horrific procedure in which the egg, bombarded by alcohol, X rays, and interrupted growth, responds by "budding" into as many as ninety-six identical human embryos. When asked, as the reader might, why this is of benefit, the D.H.C. explains that this is "one of the major instruments of social stability." Lower caste laborers—Epsilons, Deltas, and Gammas—are produced by this "bokanovskification." He is disappointed that there is a limit to the buds that one European egg may engender. Exotic eggs, from Singapore and Africa, are yet more prolific.

In the Bottling Room we learn about "decanting," which is no less than the birth process as appropriated by the laboratory. Like the assembly line credited to the apotheosized Ford, the Conditioning Centre produces products—new human beings—that move, like automobiles in progressive stages of completion, toward their designated place in society. In the Social Predestination Room information is transferred "from test tube to bottle" and the individual becomes a commodity guaranteed to live up to expectations. Conditioned by shaking to minimize the "trauma of decanting," embryos achieve independent existence outside "the realm of mere slavish imitation of nature into the much more interesting world of human invention." The D.H.C., as Huxley's ironic voice, fulfills the prerogative of the genre of satire to suggest the outrageous and the obligation of the satirist to invent a world that may shock us, but that we cannot fail to recognize.

"Happiness and virtue" reside in social conditioning. The students, already conditioned themselves, and we, the readers, seeming to stand alongside them, watch as Beta technician Lenina Crowne inoculates several embryos, destined to work in the tropics, against typhoid and sleeping sickness. A comical aspect of satire lies in the complicity of the reader. Of course, we cannot act upon the literature. As readers, we may only stop reading in protest. Because we already recognize social and scientific progress and may believe it inevitable, if not always beneficial, Huxley engages both our curiosity and our helplessness to resist narrative movement. We hide quietly among the students.

The appalling neo-Pavlovian conditioning rooms have efficiently replaced all manner of parenting styles. Sunlight, emerging from behind a cloud, "transfigures" the roses and "illuminates" the open pages of books used in the conditioning process. As in chapter one, the light intends to interfere, transform, or heighten perceptions. But the very young children in this Bokanovsky group are undergoing aversion therapy by which they will reject both nature and text in order to be satisfied in their low caste. Electric shock, sirens, and explosions ensure that flowers and books will evoke only an "instinctive hatred." Nature may never distract and inspire them, and the sunlight is defeated like a rejected and exiled deity.

Mustapha Mond, the Resident Controller for Western Europe, is introduced in **chapter three,** when he visits the Hatchery. He is the only character with both a knowledge of history and a sense of irony. There are rumors that he has books locked in a safe in his study, and the D.H.C. is nervous about "contamination" of, or by, history. But Mustapha Mond's intention is always to affirm the state. He explains the history of the World State and offers comparisons between the present and the time before the state, quickly dismissing ancient civilizations, mythological figures, the Judeo-Christian world, architecture, Shakespeare, philosophy, and music as "bunk." He describes the "squalid" domesticity of family and home in terms and images so repulsive that the reader may wonder at Huxley's satiric intention.

Huxley changes his narrative technique in this third chapter. He juxtaposes disparate scenes to explicate the direction of the novel's action and to evoke the spontaneity and fragmentation always at play within the individual and society. In this new world, however, spontaneity dissipates in programmed activity and any play between individuals is controlled by the strictest morality and a constant supply of the narcotic soma. As Mustapha Mond brushes history away like "a little dust," Hatchery workers plan their leisure-time activities. They consider the "feelies," films that engage viewers' passive physical responses. By electronically reproducing responses to correspond with filmed images, the feelies substitute sensation for action. Mustapha Mond asks the D.H.C. and Bernard Marx to imagine the repugnant idea of life begun by a "viviparous mother." He describes the "obscene relationships" within families in the time before the World State; elsewhere, Lenina Crowne, a perfectly conditioned Beta, reviews the instructions on her birth control pills. "Our Ford—or Our Freud," as he had called himself, warned of the dangers of the family, the controller continues. Fathers caused unspecified "misery." Mothers, on the other hand, were the source of every problem from "sadism to chastity." This is a familiar lesson, a reinforcing drill. "Hypnopaedic" proverbs (proverbs repeated over and over again at night) remind the citizen that "every one belongs to every one else." "No wonder these pre-moderns were mad," Mustapha Mond remarks. But, when Bernard Marx hears comments praising Lenina's sexual value, he feels antisocial outrage that she may be so reduced to "a bit of meat." Meanwhile, Lenina mentions Bernard Marx, the moody Alpha Plus from the psychology department, as a possible sexual partner. She tells her friend that he has invited her to see the Savage Reservation. "They say he doesn't like Obstacle Golf," her friend cautions, and that he likes to be alone. Fragments of history, fragments of conversation, hypnopaedic aphorisms of the World State, and a biblical echo as Mustapha Mond utters an oddly equivocal "Suffer little children," are absorbed in the chapter's closing image of conveyors moving precisely forward in the light that transforms test tubes into rubies. In chapter three we grasp the philosophy of the World State in a catalogue of everyday particulars.

We learn in **chapter four** that Bernard Marx is an imperfect Alpha Plus with a physique "hardly better than the average Gamma." He is a compromised character, self-conscious, dissatisfied, and suspicious of his sexual adequacy. There is speculation that he was "mistaken for a Gamma" and that alcohol was added to his embryonic solutions. Shorter and less attractive than the others of his caste, he imagines resistance to his authority among the lower orders and contempt among his equals. He feels "wretched" after a confrontation with a puzzled Lenina Crowne in which he criticizes her public discussion of sexual intimacy and of her "healthy and virtuous" promiscuity. Lenina is well adjusted and Bernard is not. He commiserates with a friend, a lecturer at the College of Emotional Engineering, Helmholtz Watson. Watson longs to write literature other than hypnopaedic phrases. Bernard Marx is overwhelmed with self-pity. Concurrently, Lenina Crowne and her sexual partner prepare for curiously detached intimacy. She is "bottled" against passion by a second dose of soma, yet she is ever mindful of contraceptive conditioning. Her "cartridge belt" of birth control pills is a sign of the annihilation of maternity.

In **chapter five** Huxley describes the organized religion of the World State. In this obscene and scatological episode religious experience is spiritual, sexual, and—digestive. Attendance at Solidarity services is mandatory and tardiness severely reprimanded. The president of the group makes the sign of the *T* (from Ford's Model-T) and the service begins. Soma tablets are the foundation of a ritual intended to obliterate the self within the Greater Being. "I drink to my annihilation," they chant as they share strawberry ice-cream soma. Solidarity hymns parody Christian sentiment as music touches the "yearning bowels of compassion." Harmonies lodge in the "melted bowels" and "move within them." The reader may wonder what could come next. Huxley does not disappoint. "The feet of the Greater Being are on the stairs," a group member cries. Bernard Marx hears nothing, though he must claim that he does. A voice evokes a debased Miltonic echo in the sensual image of an "enormous negro dove" benignly brooding over the concluding orgy in the "crimson twilight of an Embryo Store." (The reader may note several undeniably racist allusions in the novel.) Infantile gratification imitates psychological wholeness. But Bernard Marx remains "separate and unatoned," unwilling to relinquish his individuality to the Greater Being. Because this is satire and not tragedy, Bernard's rebelliousness is petulant, not heroic.

Chapter six, divided into three parts, is the narrative transition from a place of containment and stability to one of risk and possibility. Social, legal, and emotional mechanisms revealed in this chapter compose the matrix against which the Savage Reservation will collide in chapters seven and eight. In **part**

one, Bernard announces to Lenina that he wants to know passion. As an Alpha and a psychologist, Bernard knows that emotional balance resides in being "adult[s] intellectually and during working hours" and "infants where feeling and desire are concerned." He describes a condition that we may easily recognize. Huxley suggests that society will bend the definition of mental health to accommodate progress and preserve tranquility. Lenina finds Bernard attractive but wishes he were not "so odd."

The D.H.C. reminds Bernard, in **chapter six, part two,** that "Alphas are so conditioned that they do not have to be infantile in their emotional behavior," but that they have a "duty" to be so, "even against their inclination." He confesses that he, too, had visited the Savage Reservation while a young man, and that his woman companion had been lost and left there. He warns Bernard against unsociability and threatens him with a transfer to a Sub-Centre in Iceland if he cannot control his moods. His permit to visit the New Mexico Reservation signed, Bernard leaves the D.H.C., exulting in his reprimand as evidence of his "individual significance."

In **chapter six, part three,** Bernard and Lenina arrive in New Mexico. Lenina would rather stay at the resort with the Obstacle Golf and the Escalator Squash courts, but she accompanies Bernard to the reservation. The reservation warden warns them that "to touch the fence is instant death," and that there is "no escape from a Savage Reservation." Lenina swallows doses of soma and is thus able to respond with a benign "You don't say so" to every alarming fact. The savages engage in marriage and family life, have communicable diseases, priests, no conditioning, and no communication with the outside world. Heavily dosed, Bernard and Lenina move across the traditional American frontier from civilization into a place of savagery. Because America has always been identified as the New World, Huxley suggests that the most optimistic and inventive of societies, the source of Our Ford and the "sign of the T," may lead the world in obedience to technology and belief in progress.

In the Indian community at Malpais (**chapter seven**), Bernard and Lenina are confronted by what they have never before seen—filth, maternity, decrepitude, and disease. They observe a religious ritual whose drums remind Lenina of Solidarity services. The ritual seems reassuringly familiar to her and, at first, reminds her of a "lower-caste Community Sing." The bloody brutality of what turns out to be an agricultural ceremony makes her wish she had her soma. An odd young man in Indian dress but with blond hair and blue eyes appears. "You're civilized, aren't you?" he asks. Bernard Marx realizes that he is the son of Linda, the woman the D.H.C. had abandoned there years before. The young man, John, is enamored of Lenina, "whose cheeks were not the colour of chocolate or dogskin," and whose face displayed only "benevolent interest." Some things never change.

The contrast between the two worlds cannot be resolved. American Indian society on the reservation is corrupt and imprisoned, a sort of theme park meant to discourage antisocial thinking among the highest castes. Suffering, cruelty, and poor hygiene mark Huxley's picture of naturally imperfect human community. Hermetic and exemplary, the reservation, in contrast to the World State, is neither utopia nor dystopia, but a community that reveals the often brutal, halting, and chaotic processes of living in community. The intention of Huxley's satire becomes unclear when we ask what the reservation represents. Because it posits neither a state of nature nor a desirable alternative to the oppression of the World State, the Reservation remains the weakest and most troublesome point in the novel.

In **chapter eight** Bernard Marx asks John the Savage to tell him about his life. "I shall never understand, unless you explain," he says. In a "long silence" John recalls episodes of his life for the reader but reveals nothing aloud to Bernard. John remembers the lullabies of hypnopaedic sayings Linda sang to him in the big bed. He remembers trying to protect his mother from a man who came into the bed and then from the women (the wives) who later came to punish her. He was happiest hearing Linda tell about the Other Place, where everything was clean, babies were in bottles, and one could fly. In his daydreams heaven and London are the same; Indian deities, Jesus, Linda, the Director of World Hatcheries, and babies in clean bottles head skyward. Linda teaches John to read and for his twelfth birthday finds a copy of the works of Shakespeare. Although the book is "uncivilized," it will allow him to practice reading. The book seems to him to explain all about life.

When John is fifteen an old man of the tribe, Mitsima, teaches him to make clay pots. As they happily work the clay together the teacher sings a song about killing a bear and John sings snatches of his mother's hypnopaedic lullabies: "A, B, C, Vitamin D. . . . The fat's in the liver, the cod's in the sea." The poignant, if incongruous, scene depicts a traditional economy of teaching that no longer exists in the Other Place, by which the child is initiated into the traditions of the tribe and, in turn, becomes a teacher. In this way society, through the wisdom and generosity of age, may embrace a lonely fifteen-year-old boy. The absence of elders in the World State underscores its sterility far more than the absence of mothers. The puzzling death of decanted citizens at sixty, which the D.H.C. notes in chapter seven, may be Nature's comment upon their uselessness.

Realizing that John is the son of the D.H.C., Bernard invites him to return, with his mother, to London. Ecstatically, John quotes Miranda's words from Shakespeare's *The Tempest* and grounds the novel's title in the literary inheritance the World State suppresses. Gazing upon the flawless Lenina, John anticipates the fulfillment of childhood dreams in the Other Place his mother had described. "How beauteous mankind is," he quotes, "O brave new world."

John's movement away from the reservation into civilization marks **chapter ten**. Bernard has brought mother and son to London for a specific purpose. Anticipating the transfer, already threatened in chapter six, for his "heretical views on sport and soma" and the "unorthodoxy of his sex life," Bernard reacquaints the director with Linda, his lost lover and the mother of his son. "My father!" John reverently pronounces. The Fertilizing Room workers witnessing this obscene spectacle react with horror and hysterical laughter. The disgraced director loses his position and Bernard escapes assignment to Iceland.

Bernard has become John's "accredited guardian" and Linda embraces beauty and oblivion in soma. John is a sensation among "upper-caste London," but Linda is of no interest: "To say one was a mother—that was past a joke: it was an obscenity." Properly decanted and conditioned, Linda has become merely repulsive. John, however, is truly "quaint" and still young. John is concerned that the large quantities of soma that Linda receives will soon kill her. Dr. Shaw explains that her life is, in another sense, lengthened by the drug. "Every soma holiday is a bit of what our ancestors used to call eternity," he explains, and in any event she has no useful work to perform. The doctor thanks Bernard for the opportunity of observing an example of human senility, remarkable because it does not occur among the civilized. Bernard is gratified by this treatment of himself as a person of "outstanding importance." Jokes about alcohol in his blood surrogate cease, he receives a gift of "sex-hormone chewing gum," important officials beg invitations to meet the savage, and women are more attentive. He boasts about his sexual prowess to Helmholtz Watson, who is unimpressed and disapproving. Bernard is offended but remains "gigantic" with elation. In his report to Mustapha Mond, Bernard will not spell out the word "mother" in his remarks about Linda, and his priggish condescension offends the World Controller, who understands the World State as Bernard never will.

Touring the centre, John observes various Bokanovsky groups at work. In chapter eight he discovered time and death and God in the ritual of initiation on the reservation. In **chapter eleven** he discovers irony. The "malice of his memory" brings Miranda's words once more to mind. "O brave new world that has such people in it." He becomes violently sickened by the contrast between his naive literal reading and his new reading through lenses of ironical experience. He refuses to take soma or to participate in the public event Bernard has arranged with the Arch-Community Songster of Canterbury. Humiliated and abandoned, Bernard weeps, takes soma, and feels much better. Meanwhile (**chapter twelve**), the Savage reads *Romeo and Juliet,* and Lenina gazes at the moon for a moment before leaving with the Arch-Songster. Mustapha Mond reads a paper entitled "A New Theory of Biology" and decides that it will not be published and that its author must be closely watched. The greatest danger to society is disruption of the belief in happiness as the Sovereign Good by a suspicion that larger understanding resides outside immediate experience.

Bernard Marx is humiliated at having lost control of the Savage and at recognizing the superior character of Helmholtz Watson, whose steadfast friendship unfavorably contrasts his own character. But Helmholtz, too, has problems. Teaching a class in Advanced Emotional Engineering, he introduced his own poetry "to see what their reactions would be." The class reported him to the principal.

Bernard is jealous of the affinity between the Savage and Helmholtz. Ashamed, he takes soma to overcome what he cannot achieve by will. Helmholtz recites his poems to the Savage, who, in turn, recites from Shakespeare's *Romeo and Juliet*. Helmholtz is moved with "unprecedented emotion." Bernard peevishly disrupts these interchanges by comparing Shakespeare's diction to a Solidarity Service hymn. Eventually, Helmholtz's delight with poetry changes to cynicism. As the Savage reads aloud Juliet's anguished lines when her parents insist she marry Paris, the "smutty absurdity" of family and an assigned sexual partner is too hilarious, the challenge to moral sense is too outrageous, and Helmholtz laughs. The Savage closes the book in disgust. Helmholtz apologizes and speculates on the source of power in writing, proposing that Shakespeare wrote so well because the world was so ridiculous. "Penetrating, X-rayish phrases" must only be possible in an environment of pain and emotional intensity, he surmises. Since such intensity has been conditioned out of society and none who are sane would wish it back, there must be a way to simulate it. "But what?" he wonders. In a society based upon substitution and sublimation, anything authentic is instinctively avoided. The absurdity of his question reverberates through the rest of the novel.

In **chapter thirteen** Lenina Crowne is so distraught by her attraction to John that she forgets to inoculate an embryo against sleeping sickness. The narrator tells us that twenty-two years later the Alpha Minus will be the first death from the disease in fifty years. This intrusion into the story confirms the authority of the narrative voice. The story is at least twenty-two years old, and the reader may speculate on whether the narrator is recounting history or fable. It may be both, if we recognize them as one and the same. We no longer hide among the students.

The clash between Lenina's pragmatic fulfillment of physical need and John's desire for an imaginary ideal points toward murder. Lenina is mystified by his professions of exclusive love, his obsession with marriage, and his shocking Shakespearean metaphors. John's highly moral sexual reserve is in conflict with Lenina's equally moral promiscuity. "Hug me till you drug me, honey," she says, poetically, and "kiss me till I'm in a coma." He calls her a whore, and she seems not to recognize the term. As John's sanity diminishes, Lenina's incomprehension continues relentlessly.

John's emotions focus upon his mother, who has died in **chapter fourteen**. Grief and remorse consume him. He leaves her room and unwittingly walks into a Bokanovsky group assembling for their soma ration. Miranda's words, "O brave new world," echo in his mind, challenging him to transform "even the nightmare into something fine and noble." He grandly promises the Deltas freedom and, when they do not respond, throws handfuls of soma tablets out an open window. Alerted to the confrontation, Bernard and Helmholtz arrive to extricate the Savage from the rioting mob. "Men at last!" John exclaims as Helmholtz joins him in the fight. "You're free!" he shouts as the cash box follows the last of the soma out the window. The Deltas want to kill him. Bernard, meanwhile, cannot decide whether to help his friends or protect himself. The riot is finally calmed by the broadcast Voice of Good Feeling and a new supply of soma is distributed to the Deltas. In **chapter sixteen** the police take the three men to Mustapha Mond for trial and disposition.

By their conversation in Mustapha Mond's study and library, in **chapters sixteen and seventeen,** we learn the historical and philosophical foundations of this utopian state. Only the highest castes and savages have the capacity to consider alternatives and abstractions, but they are intellectual cripples and a manageable danger to social stability. Bernard and Helmholtz are baffled by contradictions between social conditioning and sudden eruptions of creative thought. And John may be enraptured by Shakespeare, but it has imparted to him no skills for living either on the reservation or in this Other Place.

As one critic has recently observed, Shakespeare (among other canonical writers) does not teach us to be good citizens. The violence, jealousy, and treachery that move the action of the plays compose a model of human psychology that John tries to imitate. Of course, the most antisocial and dramatic aspects of Shakespeare's characters make the strongest impression. Shakespeare, as he reads it, is culture—or it should be. John is a student for whom there are no teachers and no mentors. He represents a broken continuum of literature seemingly impotent either to preserve itself or to prevail against technology. He may also represent the danger that intellectual hunger may be defeated, like the sunlight, and turn inward upon the self, transformed into something inert and sterile.

Mustapha Mond agrees with John that, while *Othello* is certainly more beautiful than the feelies, the calm stability of "actual happiness always looks pretty squalid in comparison with the overcompensations for misery." Mustapha Mond understands what John does not. Literature is a conversation with the individual, and when conversation is made impossible, literature disappears. To insure the World State against corruption and loss, literature must disappear. Only in conditions of instability is there any need for literature or God, the Controller explains. John claims the "right to be unhappy" in a world of experience, error, and text.

The **eighteenth, and final, chapter** of *Brave New World* affirms the strength of the World State. Sad at their defeat by the pitiless Mustapha Mond, Bernard, Helmholtz, and John are paradoxically happy. Helmholtz and Bernard are reassigned to remote Sub-Centres (Bernard to Iceland after all) and John moves into an abandoned lighthouse where the beautiful view evokes for him the presence of God. Idealistic and alienated, John becomes an aesthete who starves and scourges himself to atone for every weakness. He is not isolated enough, however, and tourists come to gawk and enjoy the spectacle of his torment. John descends, inevitably, into madness and suicide.

In this fantasy of technology and order carried to extremes, Huxley juxtaposes the dispassion of the state and the individual's desire for protection from a state of nature, with the loss of the creative, individual self. The intellectual and emotional tension of the clash warns of a tendency of technological society toward fascism, the usurpation of personal freedom and goals by a seemingly benevolent state. Unable to balance progress and human need, and unable to control our own technology, we may be forced to give up more than we imagine. But Huxley gives a sign of the human capacity for recovery and growth by the necessity of soma and birth control to accomplish what even eugenics cannot. John the Savage, in effect, speaks for the dead and the no longer published, and his suicide is not a failure but a seed. As part of a story recounted years later, John may be a prophet. Perhaps hope, after all, is the theme of *Brave New World*. ❖

—*Tenley Williams*
New York University

List of Characters

Bernard Marx is an Alpha Plus psychologist whose antenatal conditioning, as gossip has it, was badly affected by an accidental infusion of alcohol before his decanting. He is unhappy and dissatisfied with the boredom of his highly regulated life. He mistakes jealousy for passion in his attraction to Lenina Crowne, and his antisocial morality comes close to implying that monogamy is so fundamental to high-caste human character that even eugenics cannot obliterate it. Alienated and self-absorbed, Bernard's moods shift from elation to despair as he attempts to control his own destiny. By World State standards his problems are pathological. He visits the Savage Reservation looking for some clue to a more meaningful existence and discovers that he and John share similar feelings of loneliness and isolation.

In an entrepreneurial act, Bernard brings John the Savage and Linda to London, where John becomes a popular attraction and a vehicle for Bernard's self-importance. But Bernard cannot control John, and the threat of the Savage's disruption of social stability eventually outweighs his value as entertainment and both are expelled from the city by the Controller, Mustapha Mond. Bernard is sent to a Sub-Centre in Iceland, which he had hoped to avoid. In his weakness and confusion Bernard suggests a tragic Everyman figure, but he cannot make a moral choice.

Helmholtz Watson is a man for whom eugenics has tipped its balance another way. He has an excess of physical beauty and mental superiority. A double of Bernard Marx, Watson's "shortcoming" has produced in him "the voluntary blindness and deafness of deliberate solitude, the artificial impotence of asceticism." He is a writer of "feelie" scenarios and "hypnopaedic" sayings, a poet of the brave new world. He is friend to both Bernard Marx and John the Savage.

Mustapha Mond, the Resident World Controller for Western Europe, has relinquished his creative self for power. Highly intelligent and focused, Mustapha Mond is, for all purposes, the World State. He is well read in history, religion, and the canon, and he has chosen power over the small amount of intellectual freedom available in a remote Sub-Centre, which would have been his only other choice. Sly and manipulative, he is alone in his region, and like a god he determines the fate of each citizen. But the State does not execute miscreants, it merely reassigns them. Mustapha Mond and the World State are nonviolent, rhetorical, and without pity.

John the Savage is a figure of possibilities and fragile beginnings. He is the son of the Director of Hatcheries and Conditioning—the result of a trip to the Savage Reservation with Linda, who was lost and left behind when the director returned to London. John's arrival in London is an entertaining scandal. He is the only character to have had a natural birth and childhood, and he alone has a history of growth and experience. John loves his mother. Like Bernard Marx, John is irrationally jealous over Lenina Crowne's promiscuity.

John's reading of Shakespeare as both poetry and ideology has made it impossible for him to live either on the reservation or in the World State. Unlike Bernard and much like some Shakespearean character, John is violent and hortatory, lashing out unforgivably at poor Lenina and causing the riot that ends in exile for himself, Bernard Marx, and Helmholtz Watson. His arguments for the aesthetic sense and spiritual ideals, though limited and inept, draw Bernard and Helmholtz to him because of their own dissatisfactions, as they will draw Mustapha Mond into conversation. He is too young and too volatile to lead anyone and is no match for Mustapha Mond. Isolated in exile, he turns his intensity to violence against himself and ends in suicide. But his story will survive in narrative, in a new history.

Lenina Crowne is physically perfect and intelligent enough to understand complex job responsibilities, but she requires constant doses of soma to live by the rules. Conditioning and impulse are in conflict over her attraction to Bernard Marx. He is attractive to her because of his oddness. Lenina is attracted to John the Savage for the same reason, with the additional reason of his youth. Hers is an unexamined life, but she seems naturally compassionate and not easily discouraged. A reader may suspect that she requires more soma than Bernard because she is innately more passionate. Female sexuality is a primary obsession of the World State.

Linda, like Lenina, is a Beta who had worked in the Fertilizing Room. Driven half mad by her life on the reservation, she adapted remarkably well to intolerable circumstances. We are meant to be shocked by her promiscuity, but we may also admire her courage and have compassion for her human need. Linda's sexuality and her repulsive physicality become her destiny. This is perplexing if the satire is meant as an unfavorable contrast between the sterility of the laboratory and the essential wholesomeness of human procreation. Like Lenina, Linda accepts effacement within the state in exchange for pleasure. But Linda is useless to society and she dies—the only character to be murdered, overdosed (with the approval of the State) on soma. ✤

Critical Views

[John Chamberlain (b. 1903) is a former magazine editor and widely published historian and critic. He has written *Farewell to Reform* (1932), *John Dos Passos: A Biographical and Critical Study* (1939), and *The American Stakes* (1940). In this review of *Brave New World,* Chamberlain recognizes that the novel is a powerful satire on technology but thinks its more extreme passages overwrought.]

So here we have him, as entertainingly atrabilious as ever he was in *Antic Hay* or *Point Counter Point,* mocking the Fords, the Hitlers, the Mussolinis, the Sir Alfred Monds, the Owen D. Youngs—all who would go back on laissez-faire and on toward the servile state. His Utopia has much in common with those of the nineteenth century—everything, in fact, but their informing and propulsive faith. It is as regimented as Etienne Cabet's Icaria, the communal Utopia seemingly made of breeding the bureaucracy of the first Napoleon with the ghostly positivism of August Comte; and its ideas of dispensing panem et circenses to the populace are precisely those of Edward Bellamy's *Looking Backward*—only Mr. Huxley, who has had the opportunity to visit moving-picture emporium and radio studio, knows the difference between possibility and actuality in popular entertainment. With the Highland Park and River Rouge plants, the Foster and Catchings ideology of consumption, the Five-Year Plan, the synthetic creation of vitamins, the spectacle of a chicken heart that lives on without benefit of surrounding chicken, the flight of Post and Gatty and the control of diabetics all behind him in point of time, Mr. Huxley has had an easy task to turn the nineteenth century hope into a counsel of despair. And like an older utopian, Mr. Huxley finds no room for the poet in his Model T. world. His poets are all Emotional Engineers.

Behold, then, the gadget satirically enshrined. As Bellamy anticipated the radio in 1888, Mr. Huxley has foreseen the displacement of the talkie by the "feelie," a type of moving picture that will give tactile as well as visual and aural delight. Spearmint has given way to Sex Hormone gum—the favorite chew of one of Mr. Huxley's minor characters, Mr. Benito Hoover. Grammes of soma—a non-hangover-producing substitute for rum—are eaten daily by the populace; they drive away the blues. God has dissolved into Ford (sometimes called Freud), and the jingle goes "Ford's in his flivver, all's well with the world." Ford's book, *My Life and Work,* has become the new Bible. The Wurlitzer has been supplemented by the scent organ, which plays all the tunes from cinnamon to camphor, with occasional whiffs of kidney pudding for discord. Babies, of course, are born—or rather, decanted—in the laboratory; and by a process known as the Bodanovsky one egg can be made to proliferate into ninety-six children, all of them identical in feature, form and brain power. The Bodanovsky groups are used to man the factories, work the mines, and so on; there can be no jealously in a Bodanovsky group, for its ideal is like-mindedness. But if there is little jealousy in Mr. Huxley's world, there is still shame; a girl blushes to think of having children in the good old viviparous way. To obviate the possibility of child-birth, the girls—or such of them as are not born sterile Freemartins—are put through daily Malthusian Drill in their impressionable 'teens. Buttons have disappeared and children play games of "Hunt the Zipper." ⟨. . .⟩

It is Mr. Huxley's habit to be deadly in earnest. One feels that he is pointing a high moral lesson in satirizing Utopia. Yet it is a little difficult to take alarm, for, as the hell-diver sees not the mud, and the angle worm knows not the intricacies of the Einstein theory, so the inhabitants of Mr. Huxley's world could hardly be conscious of the satirical overtones of the Huxleyan prose. And the bogy of mass production seems a little over-wrought, since the need for it as religion, in a world that could rigidly control its birth rate and in which no one could make any money out of advertising and selling, would be scarcely intelligible even to His Fordship. Finally, if Mr. Huxley is unduly bothered about the impending static world, let him go back to his biology and meditate on the possibility that even in laboratory-created children mutations might be inevitable. A highly mechanized world, yes; but it might breed one Rousseau to shake it to the foundations and send men back to the hills and the goatskins. Meanwhile, while we are waiting for *My Life and Work* to replace the Bible, *Brave New World* may divert us; it offers a stop-gap.

—John Chamberlain, "Aldous Huxley's Satirical Model T World,"
New York Times Book Review, 7 February 1932, p. 5

HENRY HAZLITT ON THE THRUST OF *BRAVE NEW WORLD*

[Henry Hazlitt (1894–1993) was a journalist and critic who wrote *The Anatomy of Criticism: A Trilogue* (1933), *Economics in One Lesson* (1946), and *The Great Idea* (1951). In this review of *Brave New World,* Hazlitt acknowledges that Huxley's work is a satire whose major thrust is to show that a mechanized future can lead to appalling results for human emotional life.]

Mr. Huxley has portrayed here ⟨in *Brave New World*⟩ a Utopia that obviously he would wish to avoid. It is set ostensibly in the far future, the year of Our Ford, 632. One has not read very far, however, before one perceives that this is not really Mr. Huxley's idea of what the future will be like, but a projection of some contemporary ideals. So far as progress in invention is concerned, there is very little in this Utopia, outside of the biological sphere at least, that does not seem realizable within the next twenty years—though people do go to the "feelies." Economically, the ideals that prevail are those usually associated with Henry Ford—mass production and particularly mass consumption. ⟨. . .⟩ The official religion is Fordianity: people under stress of emotion say "Ford forbid!" or "Ford's in his flivver; all's well with the world," and make the sign of the T. *My Life and Work* has replaced the Bible, and all old books are forbidden to circulate because they suggest the past and history is bunk. Moreover, reading wastes time that should be given to consumption. ⟨. . .⟩

What is wrong with this Utopia? Mr. Huxley attempts to tell us by the device of introducing a "savage," brought up under other ideals on an Indian reservation, and having read that author unknown to the Model T Utopia, Shakespeare. In the admittedly violent and often irrational reactions of the "savage" we have the indictment of this civilization. Not only is there no place in it for love, for romance, for fidelity, for parental affection; there is no suffering in it, and hence absolutely no need of nobility and heroism. In such a society the tragedies of Shakespeare become not merely irrelevant, but literally meaningless. This Model T civilization is distinguished by supreme stability, comfort, and happiness, but these things can be purchased only at a price, and the price is a high one. Not merely art and religion are brought to a standstill, but science itself, lest it make discoveries that would be socially disturbing. Even one of the ten World Controllers is led to suspect the truth, though of course forbidding the publication, of a theory holding that the purpose of life is not the maintenance of well-being, but "some intensification and refining of consciousness, some enlargement of knowledge."

Brave New World is successful as a novel and as a satire; but one need not accept all its apparent implications. A little suffering, a little irrationality, a little division and chaos, are perhaps necessary ingredients of an ideal state, but there has probably never been a time when the world has not had an oversupply of them. Only when we have reduced them enormously will Mr. Huxley's central problem become a real problem.
—Henry Hazlitt, "What's Wrong with Utopia?," *Nation,* 17 February 1932, pp. 204, 206

ALEXANDER HENDERSON ON SCIENCE, CULTURE, AND HUXLEY'S VISION OF THE PRESENT

[Alexander Henderson is the author of *Aldous Huxley* (1935), from which the following extract is taken. Here,

Henderson notes how Huxley had always been bored by books about the future, but he argues that *Brave New World* is not about the future at all but about the present state of science and culture in the Western world.]

'My own feeling whenever I see a book about the future,' says Huxley in *Do What You Will*, 'is one of boredom and exasperation.'

How then, it may be asked, does Huxley come to be himself writing a book about a topic so disagreeable to him? The answer is that *Brave New World* is no such book. Not a future civilization, but the present is its subject. And especially all those characteristics of a civilization which is rapidly becoming what may be called a 'wrapped in cellophane' civilization. By this I mean the valuing of comfort above experience, stability above experiment, so-called science above nature. This temper shows itself in many aspects of daily life. ⟨. . .⟩

This is one of the things Huxley is writing about in *Brave New World*. His whole subject is, of course, much bigger than this. The book is a debate on a question which he addresses in the first place to himself, for it concerns that urgent personal problem which we have already seen symbolized in *Point Counter Point* in the persons of Rampion and Philip Quarles—the problem of 'noble savagery' or intellectualism.

This same question is addressed in the second place to a world coming increasingly under the impress of Western, scientific civilization. Is the spread of comfort, of immunity from disease, from old age—in short, of immunity from life—to be allowed to continue, or should we try to hold back this flood of civilization, as Lawrence thought, and as Huxley is at times inclined to think also.

'I don't want comfort,' says the Savage in *Brave New World*, 'I want God, I want poetry, I want real danger, I want freedom, I want goodness, I want sin.'

Comfort or God. That is the problem debated in *Brave New World*. A problem of the present, not of the future.

For as the world is going we are getting more and more comfort every day, and yet comfort is proving insufficient for happiness, as the Nazi revolution showed. Much of the impulsive vigour of that revolution sprang from a desire for God, a desire for real danger. The Hitler *Jugend* do not want to be ordinary comfortable men, they want to be heroes.

Poetry, which the Savage also wanted, is valuable in that it is the only way out of otherwise inescapable situations. But as the number of inescapable situations diminishes, so will the need for poetry. Given time, almost everything except death is now escapable. Hence one may either relieve the emotions by thinking that to-morrow will be different, and going to see a psycho-analyst, or by writing a poem. In an age disposed to be scientific, clinical, curative, we prefer time to poetry. We would rather a permanganate-of-potash treatment than a dozen sonnets on the vanities of the flesh.

The need for poetry is going, that for God has largely gone, there is little real danger, little sense of sin, a diminishing amount of freedom, and perhaps too a cooling-off in goodness. Shall we let these things go, do we really prefer comfort? *Brave New World* considers this question from every angle. Brilliantly coloured and lit, the characters symbolizing this problem move before us in a ballet at once farcical and tragic. For if we do want God, and danger, and poetry and sin, are we at the same time prepared to claim the right to be unhappy—'Not to mention the right to grow old and ugly and impotent; the right to have syphilis and cancer; the right to have too little to eat; the right to be lousy; the right to live in constant apprehension of what may happen to-morrow; the right to catch typhoid; the right to be tortured by unspeakable pains of every kind.'

We have to consider whether we are prepared to accept all these things along with the poetry and God.

In *Brave New World* the Savage alone claims them all.
—Alexander Henderson, *Aldous Huxley* (London: Chatto & Windus, 1935), pp. 87–90

[Aldous Huxley wrote a preface to a 1946 edition of *Brave New World* in which he supplies his reflections on the writing of the work and its import. Here, Huxley ruminates on the nature of the totalitarian state, believing that a critical function of a dictator is to make his subjects reconciled to their fate.]

A really efficient totalitarian state would be one in which the all-powerful executive of political bosses and their army of managers control a population of slaves who do not have to be coerced, because they love their servitude. ⟨. . .⟩ The love of servitude cannot be established except as the result of a deep, personal revolution in human minds and bodies. To bring about that revolution we require, among others, the following discoveries and inventions. First, a greatly improved technique of suggestion—through infant conditioning and, later, with the aid of drugs, such as scopolamine. Second, a fully developed science of human differences, enabling government managers to assign any given individual to his or her proper place in the social and economic hierarchy. (Round pegs in square holes tend to have dangerous thoughts about the social system and to infect others with their discontents.) Third (since reality, however utopian, is something from which people feel the need of taking pretty frequent holidays), a substitute for alcohol and the other narcotics, something at once less harmful and more pleasure-giving than gin or heroin. And fourth (but this would be a long-term project, which it would take generations of totalitarian control to bring to a successful conclusion) a foolproof system of eugenics, designed to standardize the human product and so to facilitate the task of the managers. In *Brave New World* this standardization of the human product has been pushed to fantastic, though not perhaps impossible, extremes. Technologically and ideologically we are still a long way from bottled babies and Bokanovsky groups of semi-morons. But by A.F. 600, who knows what may not be happening? Meanwhile the other characteristic features of that happier and more stable world—the equivalents of soma and hypnopaedia and the scientific caste system—are probably not more than three or four generations away. Nor does the sexual promiscuity of *Brave*

New World seem so very distant. There are already certain American cities in which the number of divorces is equal to the number of marriages. In a few years, no doubt, marriage licenses will be sold like dog licenses, good for a period of twelve months, with no law against changing dogs or keeping more than one animal at a time. As political and economic freedom diminishes, sexual freedom tends compensatingly to increase. And the dictator (unless he needs cannon fodder and families with which to colonize empty or conquered territories) will do well to encourage that freedom. In conjunction with the freedom to daydream under the influence of dope and movies and the radio, it will help to reconcile his subjects to the servitude which is their fate.

> —Aldous Huxley, "Foreword," *Brave New World* (New York: Harper & Brothers, 1946), pp. xvi–xix

GEORGE ORWELL ON THE LACK OF MOTIVATION IN *BRAVE NEW WORLD*

[George Orwell, the pseudonym of Eric Blair (1903–1950), was a prolific British essayist, critic, and novelist, and author of two pioneering works of fiction, *Animal Farm* (1945) and *Nineteen Eighty-four* (1949), to which *Brave New World* is frequently compared. In the following review of E. I. Zamyatin's dystopian novel *We*, Orwell briefly addresses Huxley's novel, claiming that Huxley has not sufficiently pondered the question of why his future society has taken the form it has.]

The first thing anyone would notice about ⟨E. I. Zamyatin's⟩ *We* is the fact—never pointed out, I believe—that Aldous Huxley's *Brave New World* must be partly derived from it. Both books deal with the rebellion of the primitive human spirit against a rationalised, mechanised, painless world, and both stories are supposed to take place about six hundred years hence. The atmosphere of the two books is similar, and it is roughly speaking the same kind of society that is being described, though Huxley's book shows less political awareness and is more influenced by recent biological and psychological theories. ⟨. . .⟩

⟨. . .⟩ In Huxley's book the problem of "human nature" is in a sense solved, because it assumes that by pre-natal treatment, drugs and hypnotic suggestion the human organism can be specialised in any way that is desired. A first-rate scientific worker is as easily produced as an Epsilon semi-moron, and in either case the vestiges of primitive instincts, such as maternal feeling or the desire for liberty, are easily dealt with. At the same time no clear reason is given why society should be stratified in the elaborate way that is described. The aim is not economic exploitation, but the desire to bully and dominate does not seem to be a motive either. There is no power hunger, no sadism, no hardness of any kind. Those at the top have no strong motive for staying at the top, and though everyone is happy in a vacuous way, life has become so pointless that it is difficult to believe that such a society could endure.

> —George Orwell, [Review of *We* by E. I. Zamyatin] (1946), *Collected Essays, Journalism and Letters,* ed. Sonia Orwell and Ian Angus (New York: Harcourt, Brace & World, 1968), Vol. 4, pp. 72–73

JOHN ATKINS ON HUXLEY'S VIEW OF SOCIETY AND DRUGS

[John Atkins (b. 1916), a lecturer, novelist, and journalist, has written many critical biographies, including *Graham Greene* (1957) and *J. B. Priestley: The Last of the Sages* (1981). In this extract, taken from *Aldous Huxley: A Literary Study* (1956), Atkins explores Huxley's use of the drug "soma" in *Brave New World*.]

For some years Huxley had been considering the possibility of a drug being used which would give the illusion of well-being without unpleasant consequences. However agreeable to the individual it might be, it would also be of immense political utility, for good or for ill. In "Wanted, A New Pleasure" *(Music at Night)* he had said that such a drug, a more efficient and less harmful substitute for alcohol and cocaine, would actually solve our problems by making paradise accessible whenever required. After the publication of *Brave New World* he returned to this idea in *The Olive Tree.* Writing of the propaganda of the future, he said that the chemist might be brought in to assist the writer with the help of chloral and scopolamine. Under the influence of these drugs a person becomes highly suggestible, and even a permanent modification of habitual modes of thought and feeling might be effected. In Vedic mythology Indra had become one with the drug, and was the mediator between the human and the divine. Later Huxley carried out a personal test with mescalin, the American Indian peyotl, which induced a state of alienation from the self. The purpose and character of these various drugs were different, but in one thing they were alike—the power to modify human consciousness. The drug may be used as a short cut to the visionary world or as an instrument for creating a loving solidarity.

Self-denial, one of the old virtues, stood in the way of a successful industrial civilisation. It was replaced by self-indulgence up to the limits imposed by hygiene and economics. In this way, for the first time in history, the demands of industry and of personal happiness coincided. In the great re-casting of values that had taken place, happiness was given precedence over truth. The paradox was that science, which had made this civilisation possible, had to be carefully controlled and only applied to immediate problems. To allow science to be used as a weapon in a never-ending search for truth would be to pass the death-sentence on stability.

However scientific the basis of the civilisation, religion could not be set aside. As Huxley had remarked so often in his other writings, the religious impulse existed and could not be eliminated. And in any case, science was degenerating into pseudo-science, and had lost its former creative power. It had become a watchdog, a Defender of the Status Quo. Any new advance that might be made was purely local, the refinement of known processes. Complementary to science in its role as social refrigerator was the worship of Our Ford, whose spirit used to descend, accompanied by palpable footsteps, upon his devotees who had achieved consummation in a Solidarity Service. Unorthodoxy was the unforgivable crime. No brilliance could forgive it—in fact, the greater the talent the more dangerous the unorthodoxy it served. Murder killed the individual, which was nothing. Unorthodoxy threatened society itself. No-one was allowed to consider the purpose of existence—nor, of course, would any properly conditioned person think of doing so. Once there was a loss of faith in happiness as the Sovereign Good, society would be shaken to its foundations. There was no tragedy in the Brave New World because tragedy was the fruit of social instability. "People are happy," said the Controller. "They get what they want, and they never want what they can't get. They're well off; they're safe; they're never ill; they're not afraid of death; they're blissfully ignorant of passion and old age; they're plagued with no mothers or fathers; they've got no wives, or children, or lovers to feel strongly about; they're so conditioned that they practically can't help behaving as they ought to behave. And if anything should go wrong, there's soma."

This world, however brave and new, was not quite one hundred per cent. efficient. Sometimes there was an accident in conditioning and the resultant individual was not completely satisfied with his lot and, worse, upset others. There was also an Indian Reservation which had not been considered worth the expense of integrating into the grand scheme, and here lived the savages in all their traditional squalor and pre-scientific bestiality. One of them was brought to London as an exhibit. Instead of surrendering to the charm of civilisation, he revolted against it, retired into the country to live in remorse and self-punishment, and finally committed suicide. In a Foreword to a new edition, published in 1946, Huxley wrote that he regarded it as a fault that he had left the Savage only the two alternatives, between "an insane life in Utopia, or the life of a primitive in an Indian village." At the time of writing *Brave New World* he found the choice amusing—for the author in those days was a "Pyrrhonic aesthete." Today he believes that sanity is possible. This is a measure of his own development, for the objective situation in 1946 seemed even less encouraging than it had been in 1932. There is no mention in the novel of nuclear fission, which today is regarded as the greatest threat to man's future. But his concern was not with the advance of science but with its effect on human beings. Advances in biology, physiology and psychology seemed much more relevant for this purpose.

> —John Atkins, *Aldous Huxley: A Literary Study* (London: John Calder, 1956), pp. 211–13

RUDOLF B. SCHMERL ON HUXLEY AS FANTASIST

[Rudolf B. Schmerl, a member of the Office of Research Administration at the University of Michigan, is the coauthor of *Course X: A Left Field Guide to Freshman English* (1970). In this extract, Schmerl studies Huxley's structural and narrative techniques in creating the fantastic world of *Brave New World*.]

Fantasy may be defined as the deliberate presentation of improbabilities through any one of four methods—the use of unverifiable time, place, characters, or devices—to a typical reader within a culture whose level of sophistication will enable that reader to recognize the improbabilities. *Brave New World* employs two of the methods of fantasy, unverifiable time and devices; *Ape and Essence,* unverifiable time only.

The choice of time rather than space as the method through which a fantasy achieves its distance from reality confronts the fantasist with a problem the alternate choice avoids. A reader does not require an explanation of the origin of the differences between Lilliput and London or Mars and Los Angeles. The fantasist can rely on the common observation that what is far away is likely to be different, and no one will ask pedantic questions about the evolution of Martian species. But what is far away in time is something else again. Time is almost always used in a forward direction by a fantasist (to go backwards, unless he goes back very far indeed, means to wrestle with the quite different problems of the historical novel), and the gap between the present and that point in the future at which the fantasy begins is not at all like the spatial gap between London and Lilliput or Los Angeles and Mars. Between London and Lilliput there is a great deal of water, and between Los Angeles and Mars, a great deal of space, and neither ocean necessitates explication. But what is between 1932 A.D. (when *Brave New World* was published) and 632 A.F. (when the fantasy begins)? The opening three chapters of *Brave New World* are designed to answer this question while simultaneously setting the stage for what is to follow.

Huxley's technique in these opening chapters has been described both as poetic and dramatic, largely because Mustapha's lecture to the students is intermixed with bits of dialogue and internal monologue on the part of various staff members of the central London Hatchery and Conditioning Centre, as well as with scenes, past and present, which illustrate what is being talked about. There is another way, however, to regard Huxley's technique here, and that is as fantastic historiography. All the action of the first chapter takes place in the Fertilizing Room, the Bottling Room, the Embryo Store, and the Social Predestination Room of the Hatchery and Conditioning Centre—and in that order. When the Director of the Hatchery tells the students that he will "begin at the beginning," Huxley chooses not only the logical start for the Director's lecture but also the logical beginning of an account of the society of the brave new world. Huxley begins, in other words, with biology, and with the very beginnings of biology at that. But he describes no more than is relevant to his theme: the first chapter ends as the students are on their way to the Decanting Room, and the second chapter opens as they go to the Neo-Pavlovian Conditioning Rooms of the Infant Nurseries. The Decanting Room represents a biological technicality not really germane to an introduction to the World State, and is thus properly left in the void between the first two chapters.

The theme of the first chapter is the biological foundation of the World State; the theme of the second, the psychological super-structure erected on that foundation. In the Director's account of the reasons for, and the practice of, hypnopaedic indoctrination, Huxley begins to interweave historical flashbacks. The suggestion is that these flashbacks are evoked in the students' minds by the Director's lecture, for Huxley has been moving back and forth from the Director's speech to the students' minds since they first entered the Fertilizing Room. But Huxley is also addressing the reader directly. The Director, Huxley writes, "had a long chin and big, rather prominent teeth, just covered, when he was not talking, by his full, floridly curved lips. Old, young? Thirty? Fifty? Fifty-five? It was hard to say. And anyhow the question didn't arise; in this year of stability, A.F. 632, it didn't occur to you to ask it." That is the sentence with which Huxley announces he is writing a fantasy. It is not until the third chapter, when the Director's place is taken by Mustapha Mond, that Huxley begins to shift his own role from that of alternate narrator to that of the more impersonal recorder of dialogue and scene.

Although the third chapter is one of the most unconventional stylistic pieces to be found in any of Huxley's novels—dialogue between various characters in different locations at the Hatchery is juxtaposed and intertwined to create a steadily increasing irony—it is, of the three opening chapters of the novel, the most conventional as history. Mustapha begins, like the Director, at the beginning, but this time the beginning is a matter of chronology. "You all remember," he says to the students, "that beautiful and inspired saying of Our Ford's: History is bunk." And in the following paragraph, all history preceding the time of Our Ford is swept away, history of which the students could know nothing, and is thus swept away only from the reader. Mustapha's account of the origin and development of the World State is Huxley's history of the future, taking the reader back to the present and then gradually bringing him forward again to the time at which the action of the fantasy begins. The story of Bernard Marx and John the Savage can thus be told against the background provided by the first three chapters, which means that the affair of John and Lenina is dramatically ironic in the traditional way: the reader knows more than the protagonist.

The use of unverifiable time in *Brave New World* is excessively complicated by the character of John. Bernard Marx and Helmholtz Watson could not have been enlarged into full-scale antagonists of their society without violating the conception of the novel; to suggest, however faintly, that something there is that does not love a brave new world, something inherent, that is, in protoplasm, transmitted through genes despite bottles and hypnopaedia, would imply an optimism totally inconsistent with Huxley's purpose. John is needed, then; he is the traveler in Utopia, the alien between whom and the natives no true understanding is possible, a Brobdingnagian among Gullivers. But in making John a strange mixture of Zuni Indian and Shakespearean tragic hero, Huxley introduces complications that blur the implicit comparison between 1932 and 632 A.F. Whatever Huxley gains by contrasting Shakespeare with the "feelies," genuine sexual passion with random promiscuity, a sense of guilt and honor with a sense of discomfort, he also loses by forcing the reader to look back three hundred years for values to set against the esthetic and ethical vacuum of six hundred years in the future. Not only is the reader given too many temporal periods for simultaneous contemplation; there is also the implication that the brave new world already exists, at least in essence, in 1932: that, to gauge the emptiness of the World State, we must go to the fullness of Elizabethan times or to that of a savage culture. If the implication were accepted, there would hardly be much point in reading the book—let alone writing it.

—Rudolf B. Schmerl, "The Two Future Worlds of Aldous Huxley," PMLA 77, No. 3 (June 1962): 328–29

Robert M. Hutchins on Huxley's Reaction to Modern Society

[Robert M. Hutchins (1899–1977) was a critic and social commentator who wrote *The Democratic Dilemma* (1952), *Humanistic Education and Western Civilization* (1964), and *The Learning Society* (1968). In this extract, Hutchins recalls that after writing *Brave*

New World, Huxley found a certain satisfaction in seeing civilization deteriorate.]

Aldous Huxley's favourite phrase was 'most extraordinary',
which he pronounced in an accent and intonation that sounded
most extraordinary to American ears. 'Incredible', spoken with
an extended prolongation of the second syllable, was a syn-
onym for 'most extraordinary'.

The most extraordinary and incredible things were the possibilities and performance of the human race. To see him stand-
ing in front of the fire, looking like a caricature of himself by
Max Beerbohm, reciting the latest evidence he had gathered,
was one of the greatest pleasures of my life.

In the foreword to Laura Huxley's book, *You Are Not the
Target,* Aldous wrote, "Men and women are capable of being
devils and lunatics. They are no less capable of being fully
human."

He saw around us, as he wrote me once, "the immense
organized insanity in which we must all live and move and
have our being". *Brave New World* was always on his mind. So
he wrote me that a study published by the Centre for the Study
of Democratic Institutions on automation and cybernetics had
"a sickeningly *Brave New Worldish* flavour". He found a certain
melancholy satisfaction, such as Cassandra must have felt when
her prophecies came true, in the work of Jacques Ellul, *La
Technique,* which suggests that we are living in the Brave New
World already.

At a meeting at the Centre he said, "To parody the words of
Winston Churchill, never have so many been so completely at
the mercy of so few." He went on: "The nature of science and
technology is such that it is peculiarly easy for a dictatorial government to use them for its own anti-democratic purposes." He
reminded the group that "the crash programme that produced
the A-bomb and ushered in a new historical era was planned
and directed by some 4,000 theoreticians, experimenters, and
engineers".

Though he thought the human race recalcitrant—"evidently
we have to have a tremendous number of kicks in the pants

before we learn anything"—he did not think it hopeless. He believed we used ten per cent, or less, of our capacities. Hence his interest in what he called 'non-verbal, non-conceptual' education, in psychotherapy, and in mescalin. These were all methods of tapping unused reservoirs of intelligence and sensibility. Like human ecology, which was another of his preoccupations, they might help us to get our technological *hubris* under control.

—Robert M. Hutchins, *Aldous Huxley 1894–1963: A Memorial Volume,* ed. Julian Huxley (New York: Harper & Row, 1965), pp. 98–99

STEPHEN JAY GREENBLATT ON THE HUMANITY OF HUXLEY'S ART

[Stephen Jay Greenblatt (b. 1943), a professor of English at the University of California, is a leading literary critic and theorist and the author of *Renaissance Self-Fashioning* (1980), *Shakespearean Negotiations* (1988), *Learning to Curse: Essays in Early Modern Culture* (1990), and other works. In this extract, taken from a monograph written when he was an undergraduate, Greenblatt argues that *Brave New World* is Huxley's finest piece of fiction, both stylistically and ideologically.]

In *Brave New World* the few true human beings who have managed to resist Progress are deviants from the majority of society. Bernard Marx, Helmholtz Watson, and the Savage are all oddities in a world where the average man can't stand to be alone, blushes at the word "mother," and goes through life reciting the slogans which are, in fact, his total being. It is clearly not possible to be human and part of the system at the same time, for the essence of man is seen by Huxley as creativity, free will, recovery of natural passion, and these are heresies which the Brave New World has suppressed. The only member of the establishment who has remained human is Mustapha Mond, the world-controller, who, with a thorough knowledge of society both before and after Ford, freely chooses to side with the state and helps mold it with a brilliant but perverse creativity.

Bernard Marx is an unusual characterization in Huxley, for he is not a typed and static figure. Gradually, Huxley induces a shift in the reader's attitude toward Marx, from a thorough sympathy at the beginning of the novel to a scornful disdain at the close. Marx appeals to the reader at first because he does not fit into the Brave New World, but Bernard himself would very much like to be part of his society—to have the most pneumatic women, to be admired by the other alphas and feared by the lower castes. Unfortunately, a mistake during his hatching has made him smaller than average, neurotic, and maladjusted. Marx's intellectualism, his professed scorn for the values of his society are motivated not by an insight into the meaning of truth and beauty but by a hasty reaction formation to his alienation from the Brave New World. He loses the reader's sympathy when he uses the Savage as a device to gain attention. From this moment on, he diminishes from heroic to comic proportions and is finally revealed as a coward, begging to be allowed to stay in London rather than be sent to an island of misfits.

Helmholtz Watson, Bernard's friend, is a much more sympathetic character but remains a minor figure. If developed further, Watson could have been the successful alternative to the irreconcilable Savage and Mustapha Mond, as the person who finds meaning in creativity and poetry. But Watson is apparently introduced into the novel only to point out the decline of art into "emotional engineering" and the impossibility of free expression in the Brave New World.

Lenina Crowne, a pneumatic alpha whom the Savage at first adores as a goddess and a symbol of ultimate beauty, is generally a comic figure but with some tragic overtones. The reader senses that the ability to experience passion lies dormant within Lenina, but she has been trained to experience only mechanical, "rational" responses and does not have the imagination to transcend them. To the Savage's poetic ardors she can only respond with the words of a popular song, "Hug me till you drug me, honey."

Brave New World is a remarkable novel and, in many respects, the culmination of Huxley's art. The gruesome utopian vision, presented in marvelous detail and with awesome imaginativeness, holds the reader in horrified fascination. Huxley has escaped from his self-conscious pedantry, his uncertainty, his lapses in style, and writes with boldness and assurance. *Crome Yellow* and *Antic Hay* had been seriously marred by a lack of dramatic tension, but *Brave New World* manages to achieve such tension through the direct confrontation of equally powerful, conflicting philosophies. Unlike the earlier novels, there is a very real debate in *Brave New World*, and, interestingly enough, the outcome of the debate as presented within the novel is a grim stalemate.

> —Stephen Jay Greenblatt, *Three Modern Satirists: Waugh, Orwell, and Huxley* (New Haven: Yale University Press, 1965), pp. 98–99

GERALD HEARD ON HUXLEY AS SOCIAL ARTIST

[Gerald Heard (1889–1971) was a writer and critic who also published mystery novels under the name H. F. Heard. Among his critical works are *Man, the Master* (1941) and *The Five Ages of Man* (1964). In this extract, Heard maintains that Huxley must have had genuine passion and sympathy for the human condition to write successful satire.]

Huxley's eye for foibles and his fascination with the grotesque gave him his original impetus. Boredom, as he told his intimates, was his main terror. In comparison with his own extraordinarily stocked mind and the originality of its arrangements, the information and conversation of most people seemed platitudinous, jejune, banal. He could, then, only entertain himself by studying the irrational quirks, the ludicrous inconsistencies, the absurd reflexes and reactions whereby the average person gives the involuntary lie to his dreary pretensions.

But, as he often pointed out in conversation, satire is a secondary manner of thought and mode of judgment. Satire, irony, parody: all of these methods of attack on pretense, hypocrisy, and sham can only succeed if it is taken for granted that fundamental to reality are truth and magnamity, beauty and dignity, love and courage. The keenness of his insight and the conscientiousness of his character therefore compelled Huxley to examine those primary virtues which irony agrees must be accepted. A mind as amply furnished as his was all too aware of those absurdities (often as repulsive as irrational) with which the moral codes themselves are disfigured. Was there no basis of essential virtue on which the satirist could take his stand? The artist cannot lack sensitiveness and continue creating. Huxley was an artist and, what is more, a social artist, a man constantly concerned with creative communication. Satire, when it can find no base but skepticism, must end in a cynicism that lacks even the gusto to mock. It is at that point that the artist becomes not a preacher but a teacher, not a philosopher but a prophet.

Huxley as an artist, a painter in words, fascinated with the noble decoration of the natural scene and the rich caparison (the arts) of the human creatures who play out their roles in this scenery, could not turn himself into that engineer of instruments of conduct, the philosopher. It is possible and helpful to see his life work as turning on an axis: from the pole of satire, when he foretold a Brave New World, toward the pole of prophecy, when in *Island,* as his life came to its close, he foresaw the perspective point narrowed to a lighthouse crag on the horizon, around which the deluge is gathering its dark flood to extinguish the lonely beacon. ⟨. . .⟩

Huxley was describing a future of physical health and also of the right of the individual not to be made to suffer—more, the right to differ, to secede, to have one's own reservation. *Brave New World* was not only more scientifically efficient, biologically equipped, and psychologically informed than were the societies of the Wellsian-Orwellian tradition, it was also far more tolerant: if you couldn't stand the conditioned-cumglandularized state you were free to choose one of several islands where the balance between public efficiency and personal whim was more to your taste, more in the private person's favor. No dictator to date has approached such generous liberalism—nor, for that matter, has any one of the democratic nations. Yet, of course, *Brave New World,* though it showed those doubts of science's plenary inspiration (which naturally alarmed Wells), was on the other hand more to amuse the satirist than to encourage the dedicated forecaster and responsible extrapolative planner.

Many times we discussed the possibility of bringing *Brave New World* up to date, but like all such sketches it had become obsolete because of the growth and findings of subsequent research. Also, Huxley's own explorations and convictions had enlarged. He was becoming far more hopeful about the human spirit's capacity to grow. But proportionately there waned his hope that the men in power in the democracies would cease to drift. He was not a defeatist, an escapist, or a deserter. He was certain that armament could settle nothing and, even if the democracies beat their temporary foe, militarism would win and become ever more ineptly, obliteratingly violent.

—Gerald Heard, "The Poignant Prophet," *Kenyon Review* 27, No. 1 (Winter 1965): 49–50, 57

THEODOR W. ADORNO ON THE CORE OF HUXLEY'S NOVEL

[Theodor W. Adorno (1903–1969) was an important German critical theorist and philosopher who wrote such works as *Negative Dialectics* (1966) and *Aesthetic Theory* (1970). In this extract, Adorno pinpoints what he believes to be the core of *Brave New World:* the separation of consciousness and intellect from material reality.]

In a discussion of a biological paper which the World Controller has suppressed, the all too positive core of the novel becomes clearly visible. It is 'the sort of idea that might easily de-condition the more unsettled minds among the higher castes—make them lose their faith in happiness as the Sovereign Good and take to believing instead, that the goal was somewhere beyond, somewhere outside the present human sphere; that the purpose of life was not the maintenance of well-being, but some intensification and refinement of consciousness, some enlargement of knowledge'. However pallid and diluted or cleverly prudent the formulation of the ideal may be, it still does not escape contradiction. 'Intensification and refinement of consciousness' or 'enlargement of knowledge' flatly hypostatize the mind in opposition to praxis and the fulfilment of material needs. For mind by its very nature presupposes the life-process of society and especially the division of labour, and all mental and spiritual contents are intentionally related to concrete existence for their 'fulfilment'. Consequently, setting the mind in an unconditional and atemporal opposition to material needs amounts to perpetuating ideologically this form of the division of labour and of society. Nothing intellectual was ever conceived, nor even the most escapist dream, whose objective content did not include the transformation of material reality. No emotion, no part of the inner life ever existed that did not ultimately intend something external or degenerate into untruth, mere appearance, without this intention, however sublimated. Even the selfless passion of Romeo and Juliet, which Huxley considers something like a 'value', does not exist autarchically, for its own sake, but becomes spiritual and more than mere histrionics of the soul only in pointing beyond the mind towards physical union. Huxley unwittingly reveals this in portraying their longing, the whole meaning of which is union. 'It was the nightingale and not the lark' is inseparable from the symbolism of sex. To glorify the aubade for the sake of its transcendent quality without hearing in the transcendence itself its inability to rest, its desire to be gratified, would be as meaningless as the physiologically delimited sexuality of *Brave New World,* which destroys any magic which cannot be conserved as an end in itself. The disgrace of the present is not the preponderance of so-called material culture over the spiritual—in this complaint Huxley would find unwelcome allies, the Arch-Community-Songsters of all neutralized denominations and world views.

What must be attacked is the socially dictated separation of consciousness from the social realization its essence requires. Precisely the *chōrismos* of the spiritual and the material which Huxley's *philosophia perennis* establishes, the substitution of an indeterminable, abstract 'goal somewhere beyond' for 'faith in happiness', strengthens the reified situation Huxley cannot tolerate: the neutralization of a culture cut off from the material process of production. 'If a distinction between material and ideal needs is drawn,' as Max Horkheimer once put it, 'there is no doubt that the fulfilment of material needs must be given priority, for this fulfilment also involves . . . social change. It includes, as it were, the just society, which provides all human beings with the best possible living conditions. This is identical with the final elimination of the evil of domination. To empha-size the isolated, ideal demand, however, leads to real non-sense. The right to nostalgia, to transcendental knowledge, to a dangerous life cannot be validated. The struggle against mass culture can consist only in pointing out its connection with the persistence of social injustice. It is ridiculous to reproach chew-ing gum for diminishing the propensity for metaphysics, but it could probably be shown that Wrigley's profits and his Chicago palace have their roots in the social function of reconciling peo-ple to bad conditions and thus diverting them from criticism. It is not that chewing gum undermines metaphysics but that it *is* metaphysics—this is what must be made clear. We criticize mass culture not because it gives men too much or makes their life too secure—that we may leave to Lutheran theology—but rather because it contributes to a condition in which men get too little and what they get is bad, a condition in which whole strata inside and out live in frightful poverty, in which men come to terms with injustice, in which the world is kept in a condition where one must expect on the one hand gigantic catastrophes and on the other clever elites conspiring to bring about a dubious peace.' As a counterweight to the sphere of the satisfaction of needs, Huxley posits another, suspiciously similar to the one the bourgeoisie generally designates as that of the 'higher things'. He proceeds from an invariant, as it were biological concept of need. But in its concrete form every human need is historically mediated. The static quality which needs appear to have assumed today, their fixation upon the reproduction of the eternally unchanging, merely reflects the character of production, which becomes stationary when existing property relations persist despite the elimination of the market and competition. When this static situation comes to an end needs will look completely different. If production is redirected towards the unconditional and unlimited satisfaction of needs, including precisely those produced by the hitherto prevailing system, needs themselves will be decisely altered. The indistinguishability of true and false needs is an essential part of the present phase. In it the reproduction of life and its suppression form a unity which is intelligible as the law of the whole but not in its individual manifestations. One day it will be readily apparent that men do not need the trash provided them by the culture industry or the miserable high-quality goods proffered by the more substantial industries. The thought, for instance, that in addition to food and lodging the cinema is necessary for the reproduction of labour power is 'true' only in a world which prepares men for the reproduction of their labour power and constrains their needs in harmony with the interests of supply and social control. The idea that an emancipated society would crave the poor histrionics of Lametta or the poor soups of Devory is absurd. The better the soups, the more pleasant the renunciation of Lametta. Once scarcity has disappeared, the relationship of need to satisfaction will change. Today the compulsion to produce for needs mediated and petrified by the market is one of the chief means of keeping everyone on the job. Nothing may be thought, written, done, or made that transcends a condition which maintains its power largely through the needs of its victims. It is inconceivable that the compulsion to satisfy needs would remain a fetter in a changed society. The present form of society has in large measure denied satisfaction to the needs inherent in it and has thus been able to keep production in its control by pointing to these very needs. The system is as practical as it is irrational. An order which does away with the irrationality in which commodity production is entangled but also satisfies needs will equally do away with the practical spirit, which is reflected even in the non-utilitarianism of bourgeois *l'art pour l'art*. It would abolish not merely the traditional antagonism between production and consumption but also its most recent unification in state capitalism, and it would converge with the idea that, in the words of Karl Kraus, 'God created man not as consumer or producer but as man'. For something to be useless would no longer be shameful. Adjustment would lose its meaning. For the first time, productivity would have an effect on need in a genuine and not a distorted sense. It would not allay unsatisfied needs with useless things; rather, satisfaction would engender the ability to relate to the world without subordination to the principle of universal utility.

—Theodor W. Adorno, "Aldous Huxley and Utopia," *Prisms* (1967), tr. Samuel and Shierry Weber (Cambridge, MA: MIT Press, 1981), pp. 107–10

Almeda King on Inhumanity in *Brave New World*

[Almeda King is a former professor of English at Classical High School in Springfield, Massachusetts. In this extract, King asserts that Huxley's society in *Brave New World* ultimately leads to a race of human beings devoid of humanity.]

In his *Brave New World,* Aldous Huxley presents a prophetic and dystopian view of where industrial civilization's ultimate goal will lead—namely, to the attainment of "universal happiness," which keeps the wheels of mass production turning but divests man of his humanity. Instead of art, pure science, and religion being the "sovereign goods," the civilization of the brave new world "has chosen machinery and medicine and happiness"—a choice necessitated by the demands of mass production but incompatible with the goals of truth and knowledge. The horror of man's attaining the kind of happiness which destroys his humanity is heightened by the realization that this society does not exist for man but that man exists for the society. He is a vehicle for the perpetuation of a society which has distorted human values in placing its optimum on industrial efficiency. Man is merely a cog in the intricate machinery of mass production. To keep the "machinery" of civilization running more smoothly, civilization provides man with that which facilitates mass production but is detrimental to man's humanity—comfort and happiness or "Christianity without tears."

In claiming his right to be "unhappy—to be human—the Savage protests:

> But I don't want comfort, I want God, I want poetry, I want real danger, I want freedom, I want goodness. I want sin.

He is protesting the absence of those things that make man human. He is protesting the price of a happiness which has rendered man infantile, incapable of self-control and self-denial, lacking in artistic insight and sensibility, and devoid of the desire to be objectively free and the capacity to love. He is protesting man stripped of human dignity. How happiness impedes the progress of man's self-fulfillment and works instead toward his destruction is evident upon looking at the order of this society and the rationale behind it.

In the beginning, which came at the end of the Nine Years' War—a period of prolonged upheaval and fear, people turned away from beauty, truth, and knowledge as "the sovereign goods" toward a desire for control—"Anything for a quiet life." Prior to the war, there had been a shift in emphasis from beauty and truth to comfort and happiness as necessities of mass production. However, people had paid "lip service" to beauty and truth until after the war, when "people were ready to have even their appetites controlled . . ." and, as Mustapha Mond (the Controller) tells the Savage, "We've gone on controlling ever since."

In the beginning, man's need for security and stability led him to relinquish his freedom to the World State, which in turn was to provide him with what he seemed so desperately to need at the time: Community, Identity, Stability—the World State's motto. Ironically, man's need for stability was augmented by the atmosphere and the products of an industrial civilization founded on and existing on mass production. When man placed himself in the hands of the Fordians, he had already been conditioned to desire and ultimately to need comfort and happiness—both of which further the ultimate goal of mass production—greater and more efficient production, but stifle and retard the goal of man—to become man. Therefore, a society based upon a principle whose primary and ultimate good fosters mass production but destroys man's nature is going to place the interests of the state at the center of the social order and view man as necessary but secondary. *Brave New World* presents the nightmare that results from this principle.

The goal of the World State—political and industrial efficiency—is reflected in the organization, values, and direction of the State. Perhaps the most revealing manifestation of the nature of this goal is the god of the World State—Ford, whose principle of universal happiness for the sake of efficient mass production, is the object of greatest veneration. This principle is the reason for being. ⟨. . .⟩

With his knowledge and belief in God, the Savage finds himself an alien in an alienated world where all the values essential to man's realizing his essence are non-existent. He comes to the new world as redeemer, as the only one who sees how far man has gone from God and humanity. His values are meaningless in the absurdity of a world in which man is not man and life is not life. His values are the values upon which man can begin to attain his humanity if man can abandon his "happiness"—his need for well-being—and accept the anguish and the joy of being human. Man must, however, recognize the meaning of the Savage's death as something other than "sound and fury signifying nothing."

The Savage came as redeemer and was crucified. In spite of the madness which led to his suicide, he was heroic in his protest because he protested. His protest brings to the people of the brave new world something of the quality of "the way" to salvation. His death, however, is both heroic and futile: He has established his humanity in a world that cannot understand what it has witnessed in his death. It is a world without tears, and therefore, it is a world without humanity.

> —Almeda King, "Christianity without Tears: Man without Humanity," *English Journal* 57, No. 6 (September 1968): 820–21

PETER BOWERING ON HUXLEY'S USE OF SOMA

[Peter Bowering is the author of *Aldous Huxley: A Study of the Major Novels* (1969), from which the following extract is taken. Here, Bowering investigates Huxley's use of the drug "soma," which he finds is used not for individual indulgence but as an agent of the World Controllers.]

After ectogenesis and conditioning, Soma was the most powerful instrument of authority in the hands of the Controllers of the World-State. Huxley had already speculated on the invention of a new drug, a more efficient and less harmful substitute for alcohol and cocaine; he considered that if he were a millionaire, he would endow a band of research workers to look for the ideal intoxicant. The rulers of *Brave New World,* with a similar object in mind, had subsidized two thousand pharmacologists and biochemists to search for the perfect drug. Soma was the product of six years' research; euphoric, narcotic, pleasantly hallucinant, it had all the advantages of alcohol and none of the defects, but there the resemblance ended. To the inhabitants of Huxley's utopia the Soma habit was not a private vice but a political institution. The World Controllers encouraged the systematic drugging of their own citizens for the benefit of the state.

> The daily Soma ration was an insurance against personal maladjustment, social unrest and the spread of subversive ideas. Religion, Karl Marx declared, is the opium of the people. In the Brave New World this situation was reversed. Opium, or rather Soma, was the people's religion. Like religion, the drug had power to console and compensate, it called up visions of another, better world, it offered hope, strengthened faith and promoted charity. (*Brave New World Revisited,* ch. viii)

Huxley, comparing his novel with *1984,* observes that in the latter a strict code of sexual morality is imposed on the party hierarchy. The society of Orwell's fable is permanently at war and therefore aims to keep its subjects in a constant state of tension. A puritanical approach to sex is therefore a major instrument of policy. The World-State, however, of *Brave New World* is one in which war has been eliminated and the first aim of its rulers is to keep their subjects from making trouble.

Together with Soma, sexual licence, made practical by the abolition of the family, is one of the chief means of guaranteeing the inhabitants against any kind of destructive or creative emotional tension. The appalling dangers of family life had first been pointed out by Our Ford or 'Our Freud, as, for some inscrutable reason, he chose to call himself whenever he spoke of psychological matters' (ch. iii). Once the world had been full of every kind of perversion from chastity to sadism; but the World Controllers had realized that an industrial civilization depended on self-indulgence. Chastity meant passion and neurasthenia, and passion and neurasthenia meant instability, which, in turn, meant a constant threat to civilization. Therefore life for Brave New Worlders was made emotionally easy; in short, people were saved from having any emotions at all. No one was allowed to love anyone too much; there were no temptations to resist, and if something unpleasant were to happen, there was always Soma. Legalized sexual freedom was made possible by every device known to applied science. Contraceptive precautions were prescribed by the regulations while years of 'intensive hypnopaedia and, from twelve to seventeen, Malthusian drill three times a week had made the taking of these precautions almost as automatic and inevitable as blinking' (ch. v).

Soma and licensed promiscuity would probably have been sufficient in themselves to prevent the Brave New Worlders from taking any active interest in the realities of the social and political situation; circuses, however, are a traditional aid to dictators, and the Controllers of the World-State were no exception. Instead of spending their leisure hours working out the practical implications of the theory of relativity, like their predecessors in ⟨H. G. Wells's⟩ *Men Like Gods,* Huxley's utopians were provided with a series of non-stop distractions guaranteed to ward off boredom and discourage idle speculation about the nature of things. Any frustrated religious instincts were provided for by the Ford's Day Solidarity Services, where, in a crude parody of the Holy Communion, dedicated Soma Tablets and the loving cup of ice-cream Soma were passed round. By these means the Controllers insured that the Brave

New Worlders loved their servitude and never dreamt of revolution.

—Peter Bowering, *Aldous Huxley: A Critical Study of the Major Novels* (New York: Oxford University Press, 1969), pp. 102–4

JEROME MECKIER ON HUXLEY'S IRONIC UTOPIA

[Jerome Meckier (b. 1941), a professor of English at the University of Kentucky, is the author of *Hidden Rivalries in Victorian Fiction* (1987) and *Innocent Abroad: Charles Dickens's American Engagements* (1990). In this extract from his book on Huxley, Meckier argues that it was strange for Huxley to write a utopian novel, but perhaps he wrote *Brave New World* to discredit the genre.]

That Huxley should have written even one utopia is, from one point of view, very surprising. His early novels often seemed concerned mainly with exploding outworn ideas and revealing the mutual contradictoriness of modern alternatives. Readers of *Brave New World* invariably point to Mr. Scogan's comments in *Crome Yellow* as an indication of Huxley's perennial concern with the future. Indeed, Scogan, a gritty rationalist, could sue the author of *Brave New World,* for it contains little that he did not foresee. Scogan may, in fact, be a caricature of H. G. Wells, and it is thus intentionally ironic that his view of the future contrasts with his prehistoric appearance as a bird-lizard with an incisive beaked nose, dry and scaly skin, and the hands of a crocodile. Scogan predicts that, in the future, population will be obtained and controlled through bottle-breeding and the use of incubators. The family system, he continues, 'will disappear' and Eros will be pursued without fear of consequences. At times he waxes lyrical over the prospect of 'the Rational State' wherein each child, properly classified by mind and temperament, will be duly 'labelled and docketed' for the education that will best enable him and his species 'to perform those functions which human beings of his variety are capable of performing'. Even the one prediction Scogan is less specific about is relevant. He complains that 'For us', virtual prisoners of society and its impositions, 'a complete holiday is out of the question'. He may not envision soma itself, but he is aware of his Rational State's need for it.

However, despite what Scogan says in his capacity as a twentieth-century extension of the nineteenth-century progress-oriented reformer, Huxley's early prose is full of utopian disclaimers in which he greets the idea of writing a utopia with contempt. In one of his earliest remarks about utopian writers, Huxley condemns them, as he condemns most of his own characters, for escapism and eccentricity, for an egoistic inability to accept reality as they find it: 'Outward reality disgusts them; the compensatory dream is the universe in which they live. The subject of their meditations is not man, but a monster of rationality and virtue—of one kind of rationality and virtue at that, their own. *Brave New World* is a 'monster of rationality' in which the rational is raised to an irrational power until, for example, the goal of sanitation reform in the nineteenth century, namely cleanliness, replaces godliness. Unfortunately, Huxley's comment about monsters of rationality also applies, eventually, to his own *Island*.

What Huxley's anti-utopian remarks in the late 1920s boil down to, then, is a hatred of the utopian speculations he was reading, or had read by 1930. Most of these, taking their cue from H. G. Wells, and ultimately from Bacon's *New Atlantis* (1627), were scientific. Those who foresee a utopian future, Huxley wrote, 'invoke not the god from the machine, but the machine itself'. Huxley's spoofing of the Wellsian notion that people in utopia should take turns doing high-brow and low-brow tasks: 'While Jones plays the piano, Smith spreads the manure' was just a preliminary for the full-fledged satire of *Brave New World*.

Thus although in one sense Huxley's novels and non-fiction prose prior to 1932 seemed to indicate that he would never stoop to utopian themes, in another they made *Brave New World* inevitable. One of the chief reasons why Huxley wrote the novel, it is tempting to conclude, was to discredit, if not discourage, the sort of utopian writing he was familiar with. The urge to write a literary satire on existing works went hand in hand with the desire to challenge, by means of a correcting, less optimistic vision of his own, the picture of the future that science was enthusiastically offering. In his prose essays, Huxley was thus composing *Brave New World* for years before starting the novel itself. In essays from *Music at Night,* such as 'Liberty and the Promised Land', 'History and the Past', 'Wanted a New Pleasure', and throughout *Proper Studies,* Huxley was indulging in distopian prose, from which the anti-utopian or distopian novel and eventually the positive utopia spring almost inevitably. The difference between the satirist and the writer of utopias is somewhat minimal to begin with, since the second, like the first, intends to expose the difference between what he beholds and what he would prefer to see. Once the anti-utopian novel is written, its counterpart already exists by implication. As Huxley became increasingly convinced that he had found the true path, he employed the medium of a positive utopia to explore a future of his own conceiving. Eventually, Huxley, too, disclosed his compensatory dream.

Even the anti-utopian non-fiction prose just mentioned, however, is hardly free of moments when Huxley is possibly not ridiculing scientific utopias, when he seems, instead, intrigued by their possibility—an attitude which often makes the reader suspect that *Brave New World* is not the total satire some critics claim. The question of 'eugenic reform' always has a fascination for Huxley. He entertains it in *Music at Night* as a means of raising the critical point beyond which increases in prosperity, leisure, and education now give diminishing returns. He even speaks, with apparent tolerance, of a new caste system based on differences in native ability and of an educational process that supplies an individual with just so much instruction as his position calls for. He worries, in *Proper Studies,* about the threat to the world's IQ that the more rapidly reproducing inferior classes constitute. And when, in an essay catalogued above as distopian prose, he predicts that society 'will learn to breed babies in bottles', or talks, albeit somewhat critically, of theatres wherein 'egalitarians' will enjoy talkies, tasties, smellies, and feelies, he almost seems to become Scogan.

Huxley is even more eloquent than Scogan on the possibilities of a holiday-inducing drug when he writes that: 'If we could sniff or swallow something that would, for five or six hours each day, abolish our solitude as individuals . . . earth would become paradise.' What Scogan wanted was an escape hatch, but what Huxley wants is a means of breaking down the individual's isolation within his own ego. The difference between the two positions, however, is not so clear as to make pointing it out unnecessary. The drug called soma in *Brave New World* is not inherently unsatisfactory, but rather is an inadequate surrogate for something Huxley would accept in a more proper form.

—Jerome Meckier, *Aldous Huxley: Satire and Structure* (London: Chatto & Windus, 1969), pp. 176–78

HAROLD H. WATTS ON SIR MUSTAFA MOND AND BERNARD MARX

[Harold H. Watts (b. 1906), a professor emeritus at Purdue University, is the author of *The Modern Reader's Guide to the Bible* (1949), *Ezra Pound and the* Cantos (1952), and *Aldous Huxley* (1969), from which the following extract is taken. Here, Watts examines Huxley's philosophy of humanity through the contradictory characters of Sir Mustafa Mond and Bernard Marx.]

Future man, in Huxley's view, will be dogged by limiting insights that are at odds with the optimistic expectations of Sir Mustafa Mond and other planners. Future man will continue to be a creature who knows that he must die; and no supervised visits of the young to the state crematoria will really dissipate man's sense of his own contingency. No amount of neo-

Malthusian drill in the schools will annihilate—at least in a few deviates like Bernard Marx and John, the Savage of the novel—the possibility that man is a creature who, sexually, can choose to exist for a particular other person rather than for everyone.

Bernard Marx, for example, looks at the calm yet rapturous face of a temporary sexual partner; ". . . the sigh of her transfigured face was at once an accusation and an ironical reminder of his own separateness." Nor will the pregnancy substitutes available to women turn out to be entirely satisfactory surrogates for the old, obscene experience of giving birth to children. Visits to the "feelies"—the improved "talkies" of A.F. 632—will not give the same results as emotion experienced and inspected in the separate human heart or soul. And it is doubtful that a drug named "soma" will do more than alleviate tensions endemic to man; it certainly will not cancel them. (Huxley is much indebted to the ancient Hindus in his later work; the borrowed term "soma" is an example of this debt.)

Huxley invents a story that makes these points aptly. After the opening visits to the assembly line that put in place the conditioned glories and securities of the imagined world, Huxley sends through their paces four or five main characters. These well-adjusted persons have such names as Lenina Crowne and Helmholz Watson (Huxley's malice appears in the invention of names which hark back to the chief cultural heroes of the nineteenth and twentieth centuries). There is the shrewd ruler of the "one world," Sir Mustafa Mond. There is the complacent director of the hatcheries. Less happy than these persons is Bernard Marx, perhaps damaged, as has been noted, by an excess of alcohol surrogate at an early state in his physical development.

Indeed, the behavior of Bernard, stunted in height and hardly a worthy Alpha, is the first crack in the Eden of the future. Bernard yearns for nothing less than a permanent sexual relation with Lenina—a desire that strikes this modest girl as hardly decent. Pursuing his hope, Bernard persuades Lenina to go with him on a visit to an Indian reservation. There they encounter the Savage, John, in whom, finally, center all the disruptive elements of this future world—accurately reflecting Huxley's considered estimate of what man inescapably *is*.

The Savage—Huxley tells us—is the offspring of a "civilized" woman, who many years before had become lost in the Indian reservation; the father of the Savage, as it turns out, is the director of the hatcheries. The mother has shocked both the Indians and her son by her attempts to remain "decently" promiscuous in the uncivilized setting. Over the years, the Savage has learned to read Shakespeare; and in that corrupt author—otherwise known only to the director of civilized society, Sir Mustafa Mond—the young man has discovered models of behavior and feeling that had been edited out of the minds of the conditioned inhabitants of London and elsewhere.

As the Controller, Sir Mustafa Mond, explains, the reading of Shakespeare is dangerous, "Because it's old; that's the chief reason. We haven't any use for old things here." There is no room for tragedy or even for a desire to create works that reflect the vision that had overtaken the Savage in his adolescence—the interplay of life and time and death. In Mond's judgment, tragedy does not arise from man's situation; it once arose from the instability of a particular situation—one that in the new society has been erased: "The world's stable now. People are happy; they get what they want, and they never want what they can't get. They're well off; they're safe; they're never ill; they're not afraid of death; they're blissfully ignorant of passion and old age; they're plagued with no mothers or fathers; they've got no wives, or children, or lovers to feel strongly about; they're so conditioned that they practically can't help behaving as they ought to behave. And if anything should go wrong, there's *soma*." This environment is disturbing chiefly to the rare Bernard Marxes of the happy society—and is doubly so to the Savage, who has escaped all the conditioning that makes the manipulated world a second Eden.
—Harold H. Watts, *Aldous Huxley* (New York: Twayne, 1969), pp. 79–81

LAURENCE BRANDER ON FREE INDIVIDUALS AND A SANE
SOCIETY

> [Laurence Brander (b. 1903) is the author of critical
> studies of George Orwell (1954), Somerset Maugham
> (1968), E. M. Forster (1970), and Aldous Huxley
> (1970). In this extract from that last work, Brander
> argues that in the last chapter of *Brave New World*
> Huxley examines the possibilities of preserving human-
> ity's ability to think independently.]

It has been noticed before that a study of Huxley's work is a
study of the mood of intelligent Western Man over four
remarkable decades. In these decades Western Man was nearly
destroyed and almost completely overpowered by his own
cleverness. The prevailing moods were anxiety and pessimism,
moods which Huxley shared. There was a balancing mood of
stoical optimism which he could not enjoy. The European
philosophers and writers who shared this view, saw the great
possibilities for good in the knowledge explosion. They worked
hard in the late forties, when the war was over, to pull things
together again and the basis of their efforts had to be hope in
the future. Their hopes have been fulfilled. The optimists are
just as right as the pessimists. Western Man is now economically better off than any society has ever been; and he is just as
spiritually benighted. The knowledge explosion presents him
with unbelievable possibilities of advance; and may lead him to
self-destruction. But in the sixties, we clambered out of immediate misery and anxiety and we began to get our human
affairs under control again. It is really no good saying we are
heading for universal destruction and social chaos. Or that we
are all going to starve. We have come back to the feeling
that humanity will go on existing as before in precarious balance; and we know that if we put our minds to it we have the
means of feeding all the people in the world, and bringing all
men everywhere within reach of the material standards of
Western Man.

In the concluding chapter of *Brave New World Revisited*
Huxley asks what can be done, and his answers are all things

which need doing, if we are to achieve sane societies. He would pass laws to prevent the imprisonment of men's minds. We protect ourselves by law against adulterated food and dangerous drugs, he says, so why not protect ourselves against 'the unscrupulous purveyors of poisonous propaganda' and he names public officials, civil and military, as well as politicians. Less directly, he mentions his old enemies, the advertisers. He has little faith in his remedy: 'liberal forces will merely serve to mask and adorn a profoundly illiberal substance' and a little later: 'The underlying substance will be a new kind of non-violent totalitarianism.' It is so easy to agree that this is very much what we have arrived at; that we are, already, what he foresees: 'The ruling oligarchy and its highly-trained élite of soldiers, policemen, thought-manufacturers and mind-manipulators will quietly run the show as they think fit.'

Huxley is hardly inspiring in this last word on the shape of things to come. He goes through the problems in a hurried way again, echoing sometimes the manner of H. G. Wells, who preached his sermon so often he sometimes hurried his delivery. Overpopulation comes first and today we are able to say, as he was not, that the pill looks like working. We can also say that it looks as if we shall one day be able to control sexing and then we shall only have to persuade mothers to want boys and we shall soon reduce our breeding stock and bring the population within reasonable limits. He speaks of educating farmers, but the people who want educating are those who prevent the farmers growing all they could. The world could feed itself if it put its mind to it in the way it puts its mind to wars and space enterprises. The seas could be farmed and many deserts reclaimed. When he comes to consider the vote and the over-organisation of our affairs, he falls back on general decentralisation and the old, old remedy, encourage the smallholder. Decentralisation would help: it would restore the possibility of prompt and sensible action; but it is no good encouraging the smallholder. He is too overworked to think, too tied to the earth, too exhausted after battling with the luxuriance and ferocity of nature to be free. We had much better depend on the machines to give us freedom. They work selflessly for others, and they now work so well that all men could be free, simply by following the morality of the machines. We need not be tied to them any longer; we have simply to abate our acquisitiveness and the machines will set us all free.

He denounces the 'modern metropolis, in which a fully human life of multiple personal relationships has become almost impossible' and exhorts us to 'leave the metropolis and revive the small country community'. Here he touches truth. Men do not have to be smallholders to live in the country and in the country we can enjoy the good life intelligently, enjoying our books and our music; yet always in touch with the earth which keeps us sane. Which is not an apology for commuting; that way madness lies. Our island has many areas more and more deserted, as the acquisitives clamber over one another round London, and these areas have or could easily have the services on which our reasonable comforts depend.

If our population gets out of hand, it could be exported. It is insane to let our doctors and scientists struggle to preserve the mass, when it could be exported to countries large enough for them to live on the earth and become sane individuals. If we accept Huxley's view that human society should be based on the 'conscious and intelligent pursuit of man's Final End', we shall accept that this is more easily done where silence and solitude are possible. Salvation, in the nature of things, is for the individual and the individual will go on trying to save himself. He will have a better chance if he is touched by good air and the earth. So we must be disappointed by the tepid stoicism of the closing words of *Brave New World Revisited:* 'Perhaps the forces that now menace freedom are too strong to be resisted for very long. It is still our duty to do whatever we can to resist them.'
—Laurence Brander, *Aldous Huxley: A Critical Study* (Lewisburg, PA: Bucknell University Press, 1970), pp. 67–69

[Sisirkumar Ghose is an Indian literary critic and author of *Mystics and Society: A Point of View* (1968) and *Aldous Huxley: A Cynical Salvationist* (1971), from which the following extract is taken. Here, Ghose praises Huxley's ability to narrate a satiric tale that combines his best intellectual powers with his natural sympathies and antipathies to modern culture.]

The brief review of the scientific aspect and multiple treatment, the sudden flight into meditations and theology makes it in some ways easier to tackle the plots and technique of his novels. With an introspective analyst like Huxley the plot, we are not surprised, is conspicuously absent. To a man of his temperament the normal conventions of the novel form must have been irksome. As a result he breaks, modifies and circumvents them as often as he can, perhaps not always to his advantage.

The most obvious method of construction employed by him, particularly in the early novels, is what may be called the house party method. There is a host, or hostess, usually the latter, who invites a number of intellectuals and hangers-on to a party. Luckily there is no dearth of nubile women, while even the married and the ageing do not mind an indiscretion or an occasional infidelity. Out of the crowd he picks out a person or a group of persons, pursues him or them for a time; then returns to those whom he had left behind. It is their turn now. Again he moves out after new victims. Also from time to time he brings together persons from different groups, which creates a comical or ironic contrast.

But in all this one notices, almost from the beginning, an under-supply of action or events in the novels. Instead there is a good deal of rambling conversation, and, as we have noticed before, more significantly, monologues, reflections and recourse to diary. He is, as he has himself admitted, incapable of the simplicities of the art. Unable to draw characters, and perhaps without any interest in men as men, he cannot write a novel from any one person's point of view or what happens to an individual. His novels are more about attitudes than about individuals. As though to make up for all this, the "novelist of ideas" is anxious to impose complex, at any rate preconceived patterns on the novels. These experiments in technique rarely touch the heart and are almost never inevitable. Philip makes so many notes, so many clever recipes for writing brilliant novels. Is it because without these intellectual props the novel of ideas would become totally formless? It is not to be wondered that in spite of—perhaps because of—this deliberate effort to put his material into shape the story is strangled and shows no signs of movement. See, for instance, the planned discontinuity of *Eyeless in Gaza,* which shows both his weakness and strength. But its technical virtuosity is striking rather than convincing. Many feel that it would have been much better if the novel had been written in the more familiar and straight-forward manner. But how can one spread order outside unless one has order inside, as Confucius said centuries ago, and as Huxley at least ought to know.

A plot is normally the function of a character or else it is the gift of a story teller. For many reasons straight-forward narration seems to have gone out of fashion. Huxley is an excellent generaliser of information and a commentator of the modern scene, with an eye for the comic and the fantastic, but these cannot replace narration. In smaller bits, in the fantasies, the narration too is superb, for instance, the history of Crome, and, in a different manner altogether, the history of the Hauberk Papers. The whole of *Brave New World* seems so solid because its inhuman world is after his heart, that is, his mind, the mind of the novelist of ideas. He is at his best when he is theorising, or satirising. ⟨. . .⟩

Brave New World has a very different locale. Beginning with a lecture to the students, it unfolds, with a great show of objectivity, the workings of the giant After Ford World State. Its tone is set largely by Bernard Marx, a little by Watson, and, ultimately by Savage. Also partly by the Controller who enjoys a kind of double vision, since he has known the Before Ford State also. The story of the Mexican Reserve acts as a sub-plot and is undoubtedly one of the best pieces of writing in the whole book. It gains enormously by being in the form of a personal narration. It is later on absorbed in the body of the main story, as Linda and Savage come to London. In London Savage is treated almost as an exhibit. He too on his part sees this brave new world around him and draws his own fiery conclusions about it, this place where everything is easy and nothing costs anything and sacrifice has lost all meaning. In the end he runs away from this maddening crowd and tries to live a life of withdrawal and isolation. (One remembers Calamy.) At last he commits suicide. We are faced, once again, with a sense of futility. It is all points, no counters.

—Sisirkumar Ghose, *Aldous Huxley: A Cynical Salvationist* (New York: Asia Publishing House, 1971), pp. 134–35, 139–40

GEORGE WOODCOCK ON HUXLEY AND THE UTOPIAN TRADITION

[George Woodcock (b. 1912) is a leading Canadian literary critic and author of many books, including *The Crystal Spirit: A Study of George Orwell* (1966), *The Writer and Politicians* (1970), and *Malcolm Lowry: The Man and His Work* (1971). In this extract from his book on Huxley, Woodcock places Huxley's preoccupation with utopia in the context of other writers of his generation and of his own writings.]

If any vision runs more persistently than others through Huxley's works, from *Crome Yellow* in 1921 down to *Island* in 1962, it is that of Utopia, the world where a kind of perfection has been attained, change has come to a stop in a temporal parody of eternity. As a young man he saw Utopia as Hell on earth; as an old man he saw it as the earthly paradise. The difference between the two sides of the vision derives from a change in Huxley's views of human potentialities. For the greater part of his life he believed that only a tiny minority was capable of the highest thought or—in later years—of spiritual enlightenment, yet, apart from the brief period when he wrote *Proper Studies,* he distrusted the idea of a world which the élite planned for mankind as a whole. In his final years he believed that he had discovered the way, through mystical discipline and the intelligent use of drugs, to give every man an equal chance of an enlightened existence, and so a Utopia based on a balance of the physical and spiritual, the temporal and eternal, seemed possible to him; such was the vision he gave concrete form in *Island*.

Huxley's preoccupations with Utopias belong to a wider movement, for many writers in the earlier twentieth century were turning away from the facilely benign Utopias of the Renaissance and the nineteenth century. Some followed the example of Samuel Butler in *Erewhon* by creating negative Utopias, pictures of a future which, by reason of some flaw in human capabilities, has turned out to be the opposite of the ideal worlds that early socialists and early writers of science romance conceived. Even the most distinguished of the science romancers, H. G. Wells, balanced his positive Utopia *Men Like Gods* with the terrifyingly negative vision of *When the Sleeper Wakes*. Years before Huxley wrote *Brave New World*, E. M. Forster ('The Machine Stops') and Karel Capek *(R.U.R.)* already portrayed in varying ways the withering of man's spiritual life and even of his physical capacities when he becomes too reliant on a machine-oriented world, and in 1924 there had appeared the first of the three great anti-Utopias of the twentieth century, Evgeny Zamiatin's *We*.

While *We* had a profound influence on the third of the key anti-Utopian novels, *1984*, its influence on *Brave New World* is obviously—if it exists—less profound and direct, despite the many striking resemblances between the two novels.

Both Huxley and Zamiatin see Utopia as a possible, even a probable outcome of twentieth-century technological developments, especially of the refinement of techniques in psychological suggestion. Both assume that in the process of creating Utopia man's outlook on life will be radically altered, since the stability necessary to maintain society unchanged will mean the elimination of the idea of freedom and the knowledge of the past, and the reduction of culture to a pattern of mechanical enjoyments. Both envisage the economic structure of Utopia as collectivist, and see its political structure as hierarchical, a pyramid topped by a tiny group of guardians who rule through effective police systems and conditioning techniques. They foresee the destruction of the very ideas of individuality and privacy, of passionate personal relationships, of any association outside the state. Both make happiness the goal of their Utopias, and equate it with non-freedom. Both use a passionless sexual promiscuity, based on the theory that each belongs to all, to break down any true intimacy between persons. The individual becomes an atom in the body of the state and nothing more. Even the rebellions in the two novels are alike, for in each case the hero—D.503 in *We* and Bernard Marx in *Brave New World*—is physically and mentally an atavistic throwback, and both heroes are tempted to rebellion by contact with men who have escaped the conditioning hand of the state: the hairy people who live outside the protective green wall of the Utopian city in *We,* the primitives of the New Mexican reservation in *Brave New World.* Needless to say, both rebellions fail; the unitary world utopian state continues on its course.

Striking as the resemblances may be, it is hard to prove that Huxley was influenced by Zamiatin at the time he wrote *Brave New World.* Unlike Orwell, he never admitted such an influence. And though, given Huxley's omnivorous reading habits, it seems unlikely that he failed to read *We* during the seven years between its publication and that of *Brave New World,* this appears to have affected only secondary details of his book. The essential outline of *Brave New World* was sketched already in *Crome Yellow,* and while it is true that *We* was written in 1920, and was secretly circulated as a forbidden text in Soviet Russia, it is improbable that Huxley saw a copy of it or even learnt of its existence before he conceived the character of Mr. Scogan and filled his mind with Utopian ideas.

The concept of Utopia, implicitly rejected in *Crome Yellow,* haunted Huxley as he watched the advance of the applied sciences and particularly of physiology and psychology. Utopia, he realized, was not entirely an impossible abstraction. Perhaps it cannot be made with men as they are. But science can change—if not men themselves—at least their attitudes and reactions, and then Utopia becomes feasible as a society in which men cease to be individuals and become merely the components of a social collectivity.

—George Woodcock, *Dawn and the Darkest Hour: A Study of Aldous Huxley* (London: Faber & Faber, 1972), pp. 173–75

K. Bhaskara Ramamurty on Civilization versus Primitivism

[K. Bhaskara Ramamurty (b. 1924) is an Indian literary critic who has written *Aldous Huxley: A Study of His Novels* (1974), from which the following extract is taken. Here, Ramamurty examines the contrasts between the World State, which is swiftly destroying individuality, and the primitivism that survives on the savage reservations in *Brave New World*.]

Brave New World presents the West European division of a World State founded not on liberty, equality and fraternity, but on community, identity and stability. Its capital is London, the chief administrator of the division is the Controller, Mustapha Mond by name, an alpha-plus who maintains law and order not with tear-gas and truncheon but with 'soma' vapour and hypnopaedic persuasion. Huxley describes it as an ultra-modern, sophisticated society of the year 600 A.F. (After Ford), about 2500 A.D., with *eau-de-cologne* baths, helicopter taxis and theatres presenting not merely movies but 'feelies'. It is a scientifically 'civilized' world in which motherhood and child-bearing have become social disgraces, mother and father are obscene words, matrimony is unknown, and sticking to one partner in amorous dealings quite out of form and officially discouraged. Being a 'Welfare State', the government makes free monthly supplies of contraceptives and weekly ration of 'soma' tablets to all its citizens. Women contribute their ovaries to the State Hatcheries as a national service, of course with a bonus of six months' salary into the bargain. Individuals are hatched in laboratories in just the required numbers and categories. The intellectuals needed for the state, the alphas and the betas are hatched one individual out of each egg, and are given the best pre-natal treatment. The gammas, deltas and epsilons, individuals almost sub-human, are produced through a systematic process of dysgenics by the Bokanovsky process, large numbers of identical twins hatched at the rate of ninety-six per each egg by budding. A batch of identical twins, with identical mental makeup, produced out of the same egg and conditioned in a similar way, working in the same office or factory, will entirely revolutionize social and professional relations, and form the very foundation of their national ideals—community, identity, stability. The problem is only with the alphas, that one-ninth of the population, left with the capacity to think for themselves. But even they are conditioned in the nursery stages to toe the general line and be happy with the environment. If still they find life unpleasant, they have the miracle panacea 'soma', an analeptic and soporific drug, supplied free to everybody by the state, to relieve mental tension, to subdue anxiety, to transport them into a chemically induced bliss, or, with an over-dose, to lull them to sleep. If still non-conformists exist, they are exiled to some islands, punishment-reservations for such individuals.

"The optimum population", says the Controller, "is modelled on the iceberg—eight-ninths below the water line, one-ninth above". And they are happy below the water line, the betas, deltas, gammas and epsilons. Their life is childishly simple. "No strain on the mind or the muscles. Seven and a half hours of mild, unexhausting labour, and then the 'soma' ration and games and unrestricted copulation and the 'feelies'. What more can they ask for?" A truly welfare state! And thus the Scientist-dictator rules, the almighty boss, directing the destiny control, supervising the genetic conditioning, and determining which germ shall be an alpha and which a gamma or an epsilon. Through effective mind-manipulation by means of brain-washing, sleep-teaching and chemical persuasion, people are made to love their servitude. For this happiness, art, science, religion, and everything is sacrificed. Shakespeare and the Bible are replaced by 'soma' and the contraceptive girdle.

By way of contrast, Huxley shows that in this World State there still remain some pockets of primitivism, Savage

Reservations they are called, in which mother and father, matrimony and childbearing, religion and monogamy still exist. From one such reservation comes John Savage brought on a visit to London. John is the son of a beta-minus female Linda, brought to be with child by a tragic contraceptual error, and treacherously left stranded by her lover in the reservation. John was born there. Educated by his mother, he grew up into a half-primitive, half-romantic idealist, believing in god and penitente-ism side by side with Shakespeare and the romantic world of Romeo-Juliet. John looks like a strange primitive specimen from a zoo, to the 'Londoners'. They appear to him as horrid beings on the way to perdition. He looks at these nice, tame, sexually promiscuous animals in horror. Left alone as an outcast by the natives in the reservation, he yearned for friendship and company there. In the complete absence of all privacy in the Brave New World, he craves for solitude. He feels he has desecrated himself by his contact with the 'Londoners', and in a fury of penitente-ism he whips himself. To civilization, his penance appears to be a shipping-stunt, and crowds after crowds come and beg him to put on the show again. Finally, in disgust, he hangs himself. An early morning crowd of visitors find only a dangling body with the toes swinging round— south, south-east, east . . . .

This is the Rational State. Huxley presents with masterly skill the consequences of Reason stretched to extremes, and going awry. The state is evolved for the people, but the people are not created for the state. But, to the dictator, the state is paramount, the rigid framework of some cock-eyed ideals supreme. The individual is degraded into a cart-horse. Science, accepting as truth only that which can be learnt by experiment, observation and inference, believes that happiness consists in catering to the physical and physiological needs, and the only psychological need it recognizes is the need to fill up leisure and avoid boredom. This is fulfilled through games, the 'feelies', and the 'soma' ration. For this utopian happiness, everything is sacrificed, art, science, even religion. God has no place in this scientist's heaven, the stars do not govern our conditions, the Director of Hatcheries does it. Even nobility and heroism are discarded as unnecessary because they are only the products of an anarchist society. It is, perhaps, one of life's little ironies, that even a scientific utopia thrives on muzzling up science and taking a holiday from facts. Through secrecy, half-truths, brain-washing, chemical persuasion and sleep-teaching, what Huxley calls a 'psychological slave-trade' is carried on in the name of happiness. The final picture that emerges is of a society that has achieved stability and contentment by descending to a sub-human level nearer the ape, rather than by transcending the human level to realize the essence.

When the novel was published, many readers felt that it was a grotesquely amusing tale similar to Book IV of *Gulliver's Travels.* Huxley himself, in a half-serious tone, calls it an essay in utopianism. But recent world trends show that Huxley's prophecies may become true much sooner than the year 600 After Ford. In *Brave New World Revisited,* Huxley says that increasing populations, technological advances and emergence of Big Business have led to centralization of power. This is a totalitarian trend. Mass communication and subliminal advertising, now carried on even in democratic countries, atrophy personal taste and degrade the human being. Huxley says that, with an effective system of mind-manipulation, and efficient supply of "enough bread, circuses, miracles and mysteries, there seems to be no reason why a thoroughly scientific dictator should ever be overthrown".

It is an irony of life that human beings have first evolved the 'State' for their own good, and now, for the good of the State, human beings are systematically dehumanized, a reversal of nature's evolutionary processes. True happiness consists in becoming fully human, and realizing the utmost possibilities of human achievement. To give right direction to human endeavour, Huxley says that the modern trends in every field—political, economic, sociological and technological—should be reversed. Decentralization of power and finance, smaller village communities with co-operative enterprise instead of the huge modern industrial metropolises, may lead to genuine democratization. A new set of values has to be evolved.
> —K. Bhaskara Ramamurty, *Aldous Huxley: A Study of His Novels* (New York: Asia Publishing House, 1974), pp. 92–95

E. J. Brown on Zamyatin's *We* and *Brave New World*

[E. J. Brown is the author of *Zamyatin and English Literature* (1976), a portion of which was reprinted in an anthology on Zamyatin's *We*. In this extract from that work, Brown studies *Brave New World* and its debt to the Russian dystopian novel.]

Zamyatin's first image of a modern society organized along efficient rational lines was London; and it is not surprising, therefore, that a similarity should be observed in two English writers who followed him and whose novels develop in new forms the themes of *Islanders* and *We*, though only the latter work could have been known to them.

Huxley's *Brave New World* and Orwell's *1984* share certain basic assumptions with *We*, but differ from that book in important ways. Let us look first at the similarities. Some of these are surface and obvious; for instance, Zamyatin's benevolent dictator appears in Huxley's work as the World Controller and in Orwell's as Big Brother; the "mephi" outside the wall in *We* have their counterpart in Huxley's "savage reservation" and in Orwell's "proles." What is more important and perhaps not so obvious is that all three books share an implicit assumption: that the more complex and highly organized a society becomes, the less free are its individual members. All three works assume the direction of modern European society is toward larger and more complex organization, and that the regimented world of Ford, Taylor, or the proletarian extremists will result at last in the disappearance of the individual human being in favor of the mass.

The assumption is never explicitly stated, and of course never criticized; yet it will hardly withstand serious examination. Zamyatin's strictures on England, particularly, are pointless if taken as referring specifically to England, since regard for individual liberty and the individual human person is characteristic, not so much of primitive and backward societies, as precisely of those that are technologically and culturally more advanced—England, for instance. A society that, like Zamyatin's city-state in *We*, had attained complete control of the environment would surely have reached such a level of education that the primitive regimentation he imagines would seem to be an anachronism. And Huxley's world organization can hardly be imagined if the mass of human beings are to remain on the level of vulgar prejudice and vulgar uniformity he foresees. The high level of co-operation and technological knowledge in all these states presupposes a sophisticated if not highly moral human community. That such societies should hold the individual human being as of no importance is not beyond the bounds of possibility, but it cannot be accepted as the premise of the argument, and is not borne out by the history of human societies as we know it.

All three works assume that certain indispensable human values—respect for the individual person, love, honor, and even poetry—are "somehow" (and this somehow conceals another logical trap) preserved on the lower and less well-organized levels of life while they disappear from the higher. "If there is hope for humanity," says Orwell's Winston, "it is in the proles," who have not forgotten how to sing; the hairy creatures "outside the wall" in *We* must revivify the effete automatons of the City; and in Huxley's novel the romantic theme of the "noble savage" appears in its most naive form: his savage knows the great myths, feels his dignity as a human being, hungers for religion, and even reads Shakespeare (!). There is no adequate attempt in any of these books to examine the concrete social or economic factors that would lead to the debasement of human values: they offer only an abstract argument in favor of the simple and primitive as against the complex and cultivated. Reason is of course uncomfortable with the belated Rousseauism of the three novels; but it was never the intention of the authors that reason be accommodated.

The satiric intent of all such novels was neatly expressed by Zamyatin himself in his essay on H. G. Wells. Speaking of Wells he says "He makes use of his social fantasies almost exclusively for the purpose of revealing defects in the existing social order." The same observation might be made of the three novels under discussion, all of which are legitimate heirs of the "anti-utopias" of Wells. All three present images of tendencies present in the society of their own day. *We* draws on the experience of modern Europe with its rationalized production and great cities, and on the recent nightmare of war and civil war during which human beings had indeed become "unifs." And its satire is directed also at the collectivist mystique present in the Russia of his own day, at the "planetarity" of proletarian poets and the crude philosophy of the "mass" to which Mayakovsky referred in the lines:

> The Proletcultists never speak
> of "I"
> or of the personality.
> They consider
> the pronoun "I"
> a kind of rascality.
> . . .
> But in my opinion
> if you write petty stuff, you
> will never crawl out of your lyrical slough
> even if you substitute We for I.

Huxley's *Brave New World* is a bitterly satirical image of the mass culture of his own day, which he sees as vulgarly triumphant in the future. Psychology in his utopia is debased to "emotional engineering," medicine to painkilling, education to "hypnopaedia," and the English language has become the vehicle of cheap journalism, propaganda, and advertising jingles. Music is the accompaniment of sexual orgies. The future world he offers to the imagination is one completely conquered by the "popular" journalism, literature, and music, and by the popular prejudices (including "class" prejudice) of the early twentieth century.

> —E. J. Brown, "*Brave New World, 1984,* and *We:* An Essay on Anti-Utopia" (1976), *Zamyatin's* We: *A Collection of Critical Essays,* ed. Gary Kern (Ann Arbor, MI: Ardis, 1988), pp. 220–23

C. S. Ferns on Fantasy in *Brave New World*

[C. S. Ferns is a professor of English at Mount St. Vincent University in Halifax, Nova Scotia, and author of *Aldous Huxley: Novelist* (1980). In this extract from that work, Ferns argues that Huxley's abandonment of the more realistic world of his earlier social novels gives rise to a more powerful vision in the fantastic realm of *Brave New World.*]

Once Huxley abandons his attempts to offer a realistic portrayal of society, his vision of the world becomes considerably more persuasive. Accepting the world of the distant future, or the depiction of a millionaire's quest for eternal life as being the author's invention, the reader tacitly admits the author's right to lay down the rules for the worlds he creates. Instead of aspiring to portray a world which his readers also know, and are liable to see quite differently, Huxley presents his vision as a fantasy. While parallels with the real world are hinted at, it is left to the reader to draw them: instead of insisting that life is like this, and thus incurring the resistance of readers who feel pressurized into accepting an account of reality which they do not believe to be accurate, Huxley, through his use of the medium of fantasy, is able to imply his own views of what constitutes reality with a far greater chance of their being accepted—after all, if the reader detects parallels between the fantasy and reality, it merely shows that the connections are already present in the reader's mind.

Additionally, Huxley exploits the fact that the worlds he creates are *different,* foreign to the reader's experience, to arouse curiosity as to their nature. The more bizarre the events or setting, the more eager the reader becomes to find some kind of ordering explanation, with the result that the explanations that are offered are all the more likely to be accepted. And while he overtly answers the reader's questions, Huxley is able covertly to comment on the real world, with the advantage that whereas in a realistic context his explanations, his commentary might be rejected out of hand, in the context of a fantasy the instinct of rejection is usually outweighed by the feeling of curiosity satisfied. ⟨. . .⟩

In *Brave New World* and *After Many a Summer,* however, the case is very different; in a fantastic context Huxley is able to resolve many of the difficulties created by his confused understanding of the relations between the individual and society. Indeed, the principal theme of *Brave New World* is precisely the conflict between the individual and society—a society which, because it is his own invention, he is able to understand and hence portray far more clearly. Although his view of society remains a pessimistic one, the tale of Bernard, Helmholz, and the Savage's confrontation with and defeat by authority provides the kind of backbone for Huxley's satiric vision of the world of the future which is so conspicuously lacking in his realistic portrayals of the society of the present. Similarly, in *After Many a Summer,* the story of Jo Stoyte's preposterous quest for eternal life becomes the ideal vehicle for Huxley's depiction of the worldly and materialistic preoccupations of his characters. Quite apart from which there is a genuine sense of dramatic excitement surrounding the discovery of the Earl of Gonister's journal, with its account of earlier, possibly successful experiments in prolonging life. In common with *Brave New World,* and in distinction from Huxley's other earlier novels, the narrative of *After Many a Summer* is characterized by a certain sense of direction.

Above all, however, in both *Brave New World* and *After Many a Summer,* Huxley not only recovers, but develops the cool, ironic, detached tone which was one of the most attractive features of his early fiction. In *Brave New World,* for example, there is evident from the very outset the characteristic liveliness which, in *Point Counter Point,* seemed to have been sacrificed in the interests of a more realistic approach. With the opening words of *Brave New World*—'A squat grey building of only thirty-four storeys. . .' Huxley begins playing an elaborate game with his readers, alternating the assumption that they are, of course, familiar with the kind of world implied by '*only* thirty-four storeys', with the provision of information clearly designed to satisfy his audience's appetite for details concerning a world with which they are unfamiliar: information, for example, about the absurd technological features of the world he has created, such as the feelies, scent organs, escalator squash, electromagnetic golf, and so forth. Indeed, there could scarcely be a stronger contrast than that between the wit and panache of the opening sequence of *Brave New World,* with its vivid presentation of an imaginary society, culminating in a sense of nightmarish confusion induced by the accelerating cross-cutting between the various narrative lines, and the res-

olutely drab naturalism of the first scene in *Point Counter Point,*
which led Wyndham Lewis to complain, with some justification, that Huxley had adopted 'the very accent of the newspa-
per serial'. Nor does the contrast end there: throughout *Brave
New World* maintains a level of inventiveness, excitement, and
energy which his realistic fiction never approaches.
> —C. S. Ferns, *Aldous Huxley: Novelist* (London: Athlone Press,
> 1980), pp. 135–38

ROBERT S. BAKER ON THE EVOLUTION OF HUXLEY'S
PHILOSOPHY

[Robert S. Baker (b. 1940), a professor of English at the
University of Wisconsin, is the author of a monograph
on *Brave New World* (1990) as well as *The Dark
Historic Page* (1982), a study of Huxley from which the
following extract is taken. Here, Baker explores
Huxley's philosophical development during the 1930s,
when he was confronted with such ideas as overpopulation and Marxism.]

In their endeavor to direct the course of history to apparently
rational ends, Huxley's World Controllers fostered the development of a society that cherished above all else collective stability and historical stasis. In the novel this revolutionary exercise
in control over populations and economic processes had begun
after the Nine Years' War, but in actual history, in Soviet
Russia—although Huxley insisted that traces of the same
processes could be detected in Europe, Great Britain, and
North America. Huxley associated such unwelcome developments with the New Romantic fascination with technological
progress, and yet the absence of suffering in Mustapha Mond's
utopia is attributable to the systematic eradication of precisely
those attributes of human nature that Huxley himself found
most objectionable. It is this fact that accounts for the curiously
ambiguous quality of Huxley's social criticism in *Brave New*

World. In this respect, it can be said that Huxley has created his dystopia in order to frame a complicated question in the guise of an apparently simple juxtaposition of contending points of view. A significant number of Mustapha Mond's principal beliefs, including his repudiation of history, disavowal of the value of the individual ego, dismissal of unlimited historicist progress, rejection of art, and aversion for the family, were shared at this time by Huxley. Indeed, they form the staple subjects of his satirical fiction throughout the interwar period. Mond's political and sociological hypotheses, however, proceed from a corrupted source, one Huxley will explore in greater detail in *Eyeless in Gaza,* while Mond's neurotic quest for absolute material security will reach its psychotic apotheosis in Joseph Stoyte's castle-museum in *After Many a Summer Dies the Swan.* Most important, his consuming passion for a completely regulated society involved an assault on mind and intelligence that Huxley could never countenance.

The secular and material values of the World State represent a massive projection of Lucy Tantamount's insistence in *Point Counter Point* that in the "aeroplane" there is "no room" for "the soul." Just as John the Savage is a variation on Maurice Spandrell, Lenina Crowne is a damped-down version of Lucy Tantamount, shorn of the latter's neuresthenic restiveness and sadomasochistic violence. Like Lucy, Lenina is a fervent admirer of machinery, a believer in progress, and a promiscuous sensualist. To create a secure society for neurotic hedonists like Lucy Tantamount, to purge them of their libidinally destructive drives in an environment of carefully stimulated apathy, is in essence the *raison d'être* of the World State. For Huxley this was a goal of sorts, indeed the only one he could envision for the Europe of the late 1920s. As Mustapha Mond observed, "liberalism . . . was dead of anthrax," a casualty of the Nine Years' War.

Huxley associated liberalism with the old romanticism and its stress on individuality, unlimited historical development, and political freedom. Like "history," it is a concept that has no relevance to Fordean paternalism and its monolithic embodiment in the World State. The World Controllers are not presented as charismatic leaders, nor do they require an electoral consensus in order to act. The end of history necessarily implies the death of politics in a world where the rulers have become faceless technocrats, worshipping efficiency and regulation, and administering a complex social system that has no need of ideological justification beyond sleep-taught clichés. Despite these objections to the despotic paternalism of the World Controllers, Huxley permits Mustapha Mond to formulate in the final chapters a detailed apology for Fordean collectivism, including systematic governmental intrusion into and domination of all spheres of human existence. Mond's objections to the psychological and economic anarchy that he believes informs the entire gamut of human history are essentially Huxley's, and his collectivist materialism was if not the most desirable answer to Sadean anarchy, at least a conceivable solution. It should be stressed that the sadistic irrationality Huxley linked with the society of *Point Counter Point* was for the most part a trait of John the Savage, not Mustapha Mond; and while Huxley consistently repudiated Marxist collectivism, he nevertheless observed in a letter written in 1931, approximately two years before the appearance of *Brave New World,* that "the Marxian philosophy of life is not exclusively true: but, my word, it goes a good way, and covers a devil of a lot of ground." A month later he observed in another letter that history was an incurable disease and Marxist economics merely another symptom of social decay: "the human race fills me with a steadily growing dismay. I was staying in the Durham coal-field this autumn, in the heart of English unemployment and it was awful. If only one could believe that the remedies proposed for the awfulness (Communism etc.) weren't even worse than the disease— in fact weren't the disease itself in another form, with superficially different symptoms."

Mond of course is not a Marxist; however, his ideas are similar enough, in the broadest sense, to suggest the scope and depth of the philosophical dilemma in which Huxley found himself in the early thirties. In his next novel, *Eyeless in Gaza,* Huxley will turn to the theme of political engagement—a subject, with the exception of *Point Counter Point,* noticeably absent from the satires of the twenties. Its exigent presence in the world of Maurice Spandrell and Anthony Beavis signals

Huxley's departure from the familiar terrain of Eliot's *Waste Land* and his long-postponed incursion into Auden country.

—Robert S. Baker, *The Dark Historic Page: Social Satire and Historicism in the Novels of Aldous Huxley 1921–1939* (Madison: University of Wisconsin Press, 1982), pp. 143–45

D. J. ENRIGHT ON *BRAVE NEW WORLD* AND *NINETEEN EIGHTY-FOUR*

[D. J. Enright (b. 1920) is an important British critic, novelist, and poet. Among his critical works are *A Commentary on Goethe's* Faust (1949), *Robert Graves and the Decline of Modernism* (1960), and *Shakespeare and the Students* (1970). In this extract, Enright finds both significant similarities and differences between *Brave New World* and Orwell's *Nineteen Eighty-four*.]

Parallels with *Nineteen Eighty-four* are plainly to be expected and plain to see. So are the divergences. The Solidarity Service starts ike a revivalist meeting or a spiritualist séance ("Feel how the Greater Being comes!"), turns into a conga, and ends in an "Orgy-Porgy, Ford and fun". The Two Minutes Hate involves the hurling of heavy objects at the Enemy's picture on the tele-screen, an orgy of self-abasement before Big Brother ("My Saviour!"), and ends with a rhythmical chanting in which "one seemed to bear the stamping of naked feet and the throbbing of tom-toms". Huxley's world has eradicated love and constancy, Orwell's has wiped out eroticism and pleasure. But even the nasty things in Huxley—the pre-hypnopaedic "famous British Museum Massacre. Two thousand culture fans gassed with dichlorethyl sulphide"—are presented in comic guise. The citizens get a kick out of seeing the Savage flagellate himself, where the other citizens are disappointed if they miss seeing the hanging of Eurasian prisoners. Huxley has great fun with his jingles, but "Under the spreading chestnut tree/I sold you and you sold me" is the most desolating thing in *Nineteen Eighty-*

four. Heartlessness in Huxley has as its counterpart hopelessness in Orwell.

Huxley fantasizes, lightly and shrewdly, where Orwell is telling the truth—he had the benefit of Nazism and Stalinism—but telling more than the truth. He builds up the hate and fear basic to his vision of the future until, through his abhorrence of a world in which two and two are sometimes five and sometimes three, he makes them all-powerful, irresistible. Like Huxley's embryos, his characters are predestined—to defeat and to selling one another.

When Huxley larks about, not in the least afraid of the obvious (for instance, the Director's confrontation with his—shameful word!—son, John the Savage), Orwell is grim, relentless, undistracted: no "sexophones" (how Twenties-ish!) or "Arch-Community-Songster of Canterbury" for him. There is nothing in his novel as corny—well, as undistinguished—as the account of John the Savage's miserable childhood with his derelict mother, whose "conventional" free-and-easiness is predictably seen by the savages as gross sluttishness. (Though the idea of having John educate himself on Shakespeare's *Complete Works* is a bright one, providing powerfully emotive terminology for his comminations as well as a title.) And there is nothing in *Brave New World* as solid and as truly prophetic, in kind if not in degree, as Orwell's appendix on Newspeak. Given what has gone before, Orwell's ending—"He had won the victory over himself. He loved Big Brother"—is alas the only possible one, whereas Huxley's gives the impression that the author was running to catch the post. If, instead of hanging himself in an Othello-like fit of shame, the Savage had sweated it out, he could have got himself sent (like his friends) to one of the islands reserved for heretics—Samoa or the Marquesas or, should somewhere more bracing be preferred, the Falklands. Banishment is better than vaporization.

—D. J. Enright, "Mortal Visions," *Times Literary Supplement,* 17 February 1984, p. 160

❖

PETER E. FIRCHOW ON *BRAVE NEW WORLD* AND *BRAVE NEW WORLD REVISITED*

[Peter E. Firchow (b. 1937) is a professor of comparative literature at the University of Minnesota. He is the author of *The Death of the German Cousin* (1986) and *The End of Utopia* (1984), a study of *Brave New World* from which the following extract is taken. Here, Firchow discusses Huxley's reaction to Orwell's *Nineteen Eighty-four* and asserts that in *Brave New World Revisited* (1958) Huxley was attempting to justify his own earlier novel in the light of Orwell's work.]

The only modern anti-utopian novel in English that rivals *Brave New World* in influence as well as in whole-truthfulness is George Orwell's *Nineteen Eighty-four*. Ever since its publication in 1949, this novel has invited comparison, invidious and otherwise, with its great predecessor. Orwell himself was conscious of his debt when he sent Huxley a copy of his novel shortly after publication. Huxley replied with a letter full of praise, mingled, however, with a certain skepticism and with language that clearly evokes the foreword he had written for *Brave New World* three years earlier. *Nineteen Eighty-four*, according to Huxley, is really about the "ultimate revolution," which was first proposed by the Marquis de Sade, who wished to consummate—to the most logically absurd degree—the revolution(s) begun by Babeuf and Robespierre. This is exactly what Huxley had said in his foreword in connection with the "really revolutionary revolution," but there de Sade is dismissed as a lunatic whose final aim was universal chaos and destruction. Not so, however, in the letter to Orwell. Here "the philosophy of the ruling minority in *Nineteen Eighty-four* is a sadism which has been carried to its logical conclusion by going beyond sex and denying it." This logical conclusion, however, is not based on a logic that Huxley is altogether prepared to accept. For Huxley, a sane sadism, as it were, was the starting point. On a permanent basis, so Huxley believes, the policy of the boot-on-the-face is not likely to succeed. In Napoleon's words, one can do everything with bayonets except sit on them. Hence Huxley considers that "the ruling oligarchy will find less arduous and wasteful ways of governing and of satisfying its lust for power, and that these ways will resemble those which I described in *Brave New World*." The political system envisioned by *Nineteen Eighty-four* is simply not efficient, and, all other things being equal, efficiency leads to stability as inefficiency leads away from it.

The letter to Orwell was not the last word Huxley had to say on the subject of *Nineteen Eighty-four*. In *Themes and Variations* (1950), which he must have been finishing at the same time as he composed the letter to Orwell, Huxley seems rather less certain of himself. "Sixteen years ago [actually seventeen or eighteen], when I wrote *Brave New World*," Huxley tells us, "I fancied that the third revolution [that is, the really revolutionary or ultimate revolution] was still five or six centuries away. Today that estimate seems to be excessive. Mr. Orwell's forecast in *Nineteen Eighty-four* was made from a vantage point considerably farther down the descending spiral of modern history than mine, and is more nearly correct. It may be indeed that he is completely right and that, only thirty-five years from now, the third revolution, whose crude beginnings are already visible, will be an accomplished fact—the most important and most terrible fact in human history." The contradiction between this statement and what Huxley had written in his letter to Orwell seems blatant, but only, I think, superficially so. For here Huxley is not really concerned with the substance and character of the "third revolution," but only with its chronology; not with the what and wherefore, but only with the when. Orwell was right that it would come sooner rather than, as Huxley had once thought, later.

Huxley's fullest evaluation of *Nineteen Eighty-four*, however, occurs in *Brave New World Revisited* (1958), which is so shot through with references to Orwell's novel that it might almost be called a justification of *Brave New World* in terms of *Nineteen Eighty-four*. In his comments on Orwell's novel here, Huxley takes roughly the same line he had adopted in the letter to Orwell ten years earlier, while making the same reservations as in *Themes and Variations*. Unlike *Nineteen Eighty-four*, Huxley maintains, *Brave New World* was written without the "benefit" of Hitlerism and (fully developed) Stalinism, and for that reason "the future dictatorship of my imaginary world was a good deal less brutal than the future dictatorship so brilliantly portrayed by Orwell." From the perspective of 1948, the world of *Nineteen Eighty-four* seemed very probable; but from the perspective of 1958, much less so. Soviet Russia after Stalin is no longer quite the brutal and terroristic state it had once been, and so, assuming that no atomic war intervened to destroy all calculations—and mankind—"it now looks as though the odds were more in favour of something like *Brave New World* than of something like *Nineteen Eighty-four.*"

> —Peter E. Firchow, *The End of Utopia: A Study of Aldous Huxley's* Brave New World (Lewisburg, PA: Bucknell University Press, 1984), pp. 118–20

Richard H. Beckham on Censoring *Brave New World*

[Richard H. Beckham is a professor of English at the University of Wisconsin at River Falls. In this extract, Beckham lays out the arguments as to why *Brave New World* might be the object of censorship.]

It is obvious why someone who believes in censorship might choose to object to *Brave New World*. This world is a world of sexual promiscuity, a world with a drug culture in the most literal sense of that expression, a world in which the traditional family—in fact, any family at all—has been vilified and rendered taboo, a world in which religion has been reduced to orgiastic rituals of physical expression. It is a world in which art panders to the sensations of mass communications and a world in which the positive values of Western democracy have been ossified into a rigid caste system, in which the members of each caste are mass produced to the specifications of assembly line uniformity.

Readers who have strict standards of sexual behavior, who believe in chaste courtships and monogamous, lifetime marriages confront in this novel a society in which sexual promiscuity is a virtue and in which the sole function of sexuality is pleasure, not reproduction. Since reproduction is achieved by an elaborate biogenetic mass production assembly line, the citizens of *Brave New World* do not need normal human sexual activity to propagate the species. In fact, such activity is discouraged by the state so that the carefully monitored population controls are not disrupted. Women are required to wear "Malthusian Belts"—convenient caches of birth control devices—in order to forego pregnancies. The sole function of sex in this society is pleasure, and the sole function of pleasure is to guarantee the happiness of *Brave New World* and thus assure a stable, controllable population. State encouraged promiscuity assures that loyalty to one's lover or family will not undermine one's loyalty to the state. Thus, "Everyone belongs to everyone else," and the highest compliment a man can offer a woman is that she is "very pneumatic"—a euphemism suggesting that her movements during sexual intercourse are especially pleasurable. Unlike Orwell, who in the novel *1984* placed severe taboos on sexual activity, since as private and personal act it might permit or encourage rebellion against the state, Huxley prophesizes that in the future the state will use sex as a means of population control on the basis of the psychological truism that men and women condition themselves to avoid pain and to seek pleasure.

Lest the pleasure of frequent and promiscuous sexual activity not be sufficient to distract the population and dissuade them from rebellion, Huxley foresees a culture in which widespread and addictive use of drugs offers a second means of assuring a frictionless society. "A Soma in time saves nine,"—a hypnopaedic slogan drilled into the heads of Brave New Worldians from nursery days on—conveys the message that individuals are to protect themselves from normal pain by frequent doses of this widely available and socially acceptable narcotic.

One of the most important uses for Soma is to insulate people from the effects of rapid aging which afflict *Brave New World* inhabitants after an artificially induced period of extended youth. In this "perfect" society—the future as heaven—most of the human qualities of life have been altered and adapted so that they are devoid of crisis and pain. Just as the inhabitants of this world age only during a brief period shortly before death and just as the drug which eases them through this period has no unpleasant side effects, so they are insulated against the normal stresses and tensions of family life. They have no parents to contend with since in Huxley's inspired anticipation of the consequences of biogenetic engineering, they are conceived through artificial insemination, carried in assembly line placentas made of sow's peritoneum, and decanted rather than born. *Brave New World* inhabitants spend their nursery years in state-run institutions where they are conditioned for future life. Those normal mortals who recall the pain of adolescence would be spared such in *Brave New World;* there is no adolescence. As adults, the inhabitants enjoy youth and vitality until near the time of their deaths. People never have to contend with the stress of accommodating themselves to the authority of parents, nor do they know the stress, pain, heartache—nor the joy—of nurturing and raising children.

The birth and childhood of *Brave New World* inhabitants is greatly reduced from the human world in which we daily live. After perusing the early chapters of this novel, the sensitive reader becomes aware that reduction is one of its recurrent themes, and that this reduction usually involves those attributes of life which make us most human. The purpose behind these reductions is to make all existence subservient to the state. Such subservience requires that even such basic institutions of human civilization as religion and art be sapped of their vital force.

With lives so devoid of pain and so concentrated in the physical and the immediate present, the Worldians have little need for the comfort or solace of religion. If religion is that aspect of man's culture which speaks to the spirit, then Worldians have an absence of spirit of which they are unaware. The reduction of religion is symbolized in the icon which replaces the cross as the dominant religious image—a T. The worship of a supernatural savior has been supplanted by worship of a lord of the assembly line, Henry Ford, and the sign of Our Ford is taken from the model name of one of his early cars. The four arms of the cross have been reduced to the three arms of the T.

Religion lends continuity to civilization, and so does art. Each is an important constituent of the emotional component of human life. But, like religion, art in *Brave New World* has been reduced to trafficking in sensation—slight, transitory, physical responses as opposed to the profound, sustained, psychological responses of emotion. The "Feelies"—*Brave New World's* multi-sensory version of the movies—well illustrates this pandering to sensation; rather than celebrating the ideas and emotions of human life, the "Feelies" are designed to give its participants a sensory overload of neural stimulation—the sight and feel of bare flesh on a bearskin rug, for example.

Thus art and religion are controlled by the state and subordinated to the support of the state, but the nature of that state is quite different from what a contemporary reader might expect. In the 1990s, citizens of Western Democracies see their form of government as the best form yet developed by man. As Huxley projects this important facet of human life into the future, he foresees neither Western Democracy nor its historical competitor, Eastern Communism, as the most likely political system. Instead of either he sees a five-tiered caste system occasioned through the perfection of biogenetic engineering and other modern devices of social control. Every man is created biologically equal to all others in his caste. The leisured classes are conditioned to consume, and the working classes are conditioned to manufacture what those other classes consume. Society functions almost as simply as the physical law of equal and opposite reactions.

—Richard H. Beckham, "Huxley's Brave New World as Social Irritant: Ban it or Buy It?," *Censored Books: Critical Viewpoints,* ed. Nicholas J. Karolides, Lee Burress, and John M. Kean (Metuchen, NJ: Scarecrow Press, 1993), pp. 136–38

Works by
Aldous Huxley

The Burning Wheel. 1916.

Oxford Poetry 1916 (editor; with W. R. Childe and T. W. Earp). 1916.

Jonah. 1917.

The Defeat of Youth and Other Poems. 1918.

Limbo. 1920.

Leda. 1920.

Crome Yellow. 1921.

A Virgin Heart by Remy de Gourmont (translator). 1921.

Mortal Coils. 1922.

On the Margin: Notes and Essays. 1923.

Antic Hay. 1923.

The Discovery by Frances Sheridan (adapter). 1924.

Little Mexican and Other Stories ⟨*Young Archimedes and Other Stories*⟩. 1924.

Those Barren Leaves. 1925.

Along the Road: Notes and Essays of a Tourist. 1925.

Selected Poems. 1925.

Two or Three Graces and Other Stories. 1926.

Jesting Pilate: The Diary of a Journey. 1926.

Essays New and Old. 1926.

Proper Studies. 1927.

Point Counter Point. 1928.

Arabia Infelix and Other Poems. 1929.

Holy Face and Other Essays. 1929.

Do What You Will: Essays. 1929.

Brief Candles. 1930.

Vulgarity in Literature: Digressions from a Theme. 1930.

Apennine. 1930.

Music at Night and Other Essays. 1931.

The World of Light. 1931.

The Cicada and Other Poems. 1931.

Brave New World. 1932.

The Letters of D. H. Lawrence (editor). 1932.

Texts and Pretexts: An Anthology with Commentaries. 1932.

Rotunda: A Selection from the Works of Aldous Huxley. 1932.

T. H. Huxley as a Man of Letters. 1932.

Retrospect: An Omnibus of Aldous Huxley's Books. 1933.

Beyond the Mexique Bay. 1934.

1936 . . . Peace? 1936.

Eyeless in Gaza. 1936.

The Olive Tree and Other Essays. 1936.

What Are You Going to Do about It? The Case for Constructive Peace. 1936.

Ends and Means: An Enquiry into the Nature of Ideals and into the Methods for Their Realization. 1937.

Stories, Essays, and Poems. 1937.

An Encyclopedia of Pacifism (editor). 1937.

The Elder Peter Bruegel, 1528(?)–1569 (with Jean Videpoche). 1938.

The Most Agreeable Vice. 1938.

The Gioconda Smile. 1938.

After Many a Summer ⟨*After Many a Summer Dies the Swan*⟩. 1939.

Words and Their Meanings. 1940.

Grey Eminence: A Study in Religion and Politics. 1941.

The Art of Seeing. 1942.

Time Must Have a Stop. 1944.

Twice Seven: Fourteen Selected Stories. 1944.

The Perennial Philosophy. 1945.

Science, Liberty, and Peace. 1946.

Verses and a Comedy. 1946.

The World of Aldous Huxley: An Omnibus of His Fiction and Non-Fiction over Three Decades. Ed. Charles J. Rolo. 1947.

Ape and Essence. 1948.

The Gioconda Smile (drama). 1948.

Prisons: With the "Carceri" Etchings by G. B. Piranesi. 1949.

Food and People (with Sir John Russell). 1949.

Themes and Variations. 1950.

The Devils of Loudun. 1952.

Joyce, the Artificer: Two Studies of Joyce's Method (with Stuart Gilbert). 1952.

A Day in Windsor (with J. A. Kings). 1953.

The Doors of Perception. 1954.

The French of Paris. 1954.

The Genius and the Goddess. 1955.

Adonis and the Alphabet and Other Essays ⟨*Tomorrow and Tomorrow and Tomorrow and Other Essays*⟩. 1956.

Heaven and Hell. 1956.

L'Après-midi d'un faune by Stéphane Mallarmé (translator). 1956.

Collected Short Stories. 1956.

Tyranny over the Mind: A Shocking New Look at Today's World. 1958.

Brave New World Revisited. 1958.

Collected Essays. 1959.

On Art and Artists: Literature—Painting—Architecture—Music. Ed. Morris Philipson. 1960.

Selected Essays. Ed. Harold Raymond. 1961.

Island. 1962.

Literature and Science. 1963.

The Politics of Ecology: The Question of Survival. 1963.

The Crows of Pearblossom. 1967.

New-Fashioned Christmas. 1968.

Letters. Ed. Grover Smith. 1969.

America and the Future: An Essay. 1970.

Collected Poetry. Ed. Donald Watt. 1971.

Moksha: Writings on Psychedelics and the Visionary Experience (1931–1963). Ed. Michael Horowitz and Cynthia Palmer. 1977.

The Human Situation: Lectures at Santa Barbara 1959. Ed. Piero Ferrucci. 1977.

Between the Wars: Essays and Letters. Ed. David Bradshaw. 1994.

Works about Aldous Huxley and Brave New World

Adams, Robert M. "The Relevance of *Brave New World.*" In
Censored Books: Critical Viewpoints, ed. Nicholas J.
Karolides, Lee Burress, and John M. Kean. Metuchen, NJ:
Scarecrow Press, 1993, pp. 130–35.

Aldiss, Brian W. "The Hand in the Jar: Metaphor in Wells and
Huxley." *Foundation* No. 17 (September 1979): 26–32.

Baker, Robert S. Brave New World: *History, Science, and
Dystopia.* Boston: Twayne, 1990.

Bedford, Sybille. *Aldous Huxley: A Biography.* London: Chatto
& Windus, 1973–74. 2 vols.

Bentley, Joseph Goldridge. "The Later Novels of Aldous
Huxley." *Yale Review* 59 (1969–70): 507–19.

Berlin, Isaiah. "Aldous Huxley." In Berlin's *Personal
Impressions.* New York: Viking Press, 1981, pp. 135–43.

Birnbaum, Milton. *Aldous Huxley's Quest for Values.* Knoxville:
University of Tennessee Press, 1971.

Black, Max. "Aldous Huxley's View of the 'Two Cultures.'"
Scientific American 210 (1964): 141–44.

Brown, E. J. Brave New World, 1984, *and* We: *An Essay on
Anti-Utopia.* Ann Arbor, MI: Ardis, 1976.

Chakoo, Bansi I. *Aldous Huxley and Eastern Wisdom.* Atlantic
Highlands, NJ: Humanities Press, 1981.

Clareson, Thomas D. "The Classic: Aldous Huxley's *Brave New
World.*" *Extrapolation* 2 (May 1961): 33–40.

Clark, Ronald W. *The Huxleys.* London: Heinemann, 1968.

Clark, Virginia M. *Aldous Huxley and Film.* Metuchen, NJ:
Scarecrow Press, 1987.

Deery, John. "Technology and Gender in Aldous Huxley's
Alternative (?) Worlds." *Extrapolation* 33 (1992): 258–73.

Dunaway, David King. *Huxley in Hollywood.* New York: Harper & Row, 1989.

Enroth, Clyde. "Mysticism in Two of Aldous Huxley's Early Novels." *Twentieth Century Literature* 6 (1960): 123–32.

Firchow, Peter. *Aldous Huxley: Satirist and Novelist.* Minneapolis: University of Minnesota Press, 1972.

——. "The Satire of Huxley's *Brave New World.*" *Modern Fiction Studies* 12 (1966–67): 260–78.

——. "Science and Conscience in Huxley's *Brave New World.*" Contemporary Literature 16 (1975): 301–16.

Hankins, June Chase. "Making Use of the Literacy Debate: Literacy, Citizenship, and *Brave New World.*" *CEA Critic* 53 (1990): 40–51.

Hartouni, Valerie. "*Brave New World* in the Discourses of Reproductive and Genetic Technologies." In *In the Nature of Things: Language, Politics, and the Environment,* ed. Jane Bennett and William Chaloupka. Minneapolis: University of Minnesota Press, 1993, pp. 85–110.

Holmes, Charles M. *Aldous Huxley and the Way to Reality.* Bloomington: Indiana University Press, 1970.

Howe, Irving. "The Fiction of Anti-Utopia." *New Republic,* 23 April 1962, pp. 13–16.

Huxley, Laura Archera. *This Timeless Moment: A Personal View of Aldous Huxley.* New York: Farrar, Straus & Giroux, 1968.

Isherwood, Christopher. "Aldous Huxley in California." *Atlantic Monthly* 214, No. 3 (September 1964): 44–47.

Lobb, Edward. "The Subversion of Drama in Huxley's *Brave New World.*" *International Fiction Review* 11 (1984): 94–101.

Matter, William. "On *Brave New World.*" In *No Place Else: Explorations in Utopian and Dystopian Fiction,* ed. Eric S. Rabkin, Martin H. Greenberg, and Joseph D. Olander. Carbondale: Southern Illinois University Press, 1983, pp. 94–109.

——. "The Utopian Tradition and Aldous Huxley." *Science-Fiction Studies* 2 (1975): 146–51.

May, Keith M. *Aldous Huxley.* New York: Barnes & Noble, 1972.

Nance, Buinevera A. *Aldous Huxley.* New York: Continuum, 1988.

O'Brien, John. "The Problem of Evil in the Novels of Aldous Huxley." *Listening* 6 (1971): 197–209.

Overton, R. T. "End of the Beginning." *Twentieth Century* 175 (1967): 48–50.

Savage, D. S. "Aldous Huxley." In Savage's *The Withered Branch: Six Studies in the Modern Novel.* New York: Pellegrini & Cudahy, 1950, pp. 9–34.

Sexton, James. "Aldous Huxley's Bokanovsky." *Science-Fiction Studies* 16 (1989): 85–89.

———. "*Brave New World* and the Rationalization of Industry." *English Studies in Canada* 12 (1986): 424–39.

Snow, Malinda. "The Gray Parody in *Brave New World.*" *Papers on Language and Literature* 13 (1977): 85–88.

Westlake, J. H. J. "Aldous Huxley's *Brave New World* and George Orwell's *Nineteen Eighty-four:* A Comparative Study." *Die Neueren Sprachen* 21 (1971): 94–102.

Wilson, Robert. "*Brave New World* as Shakespeare Criticism." *Shakespeare Association Bulletin* 21 (1946): 99–107.

Index of
Themes and Ideas